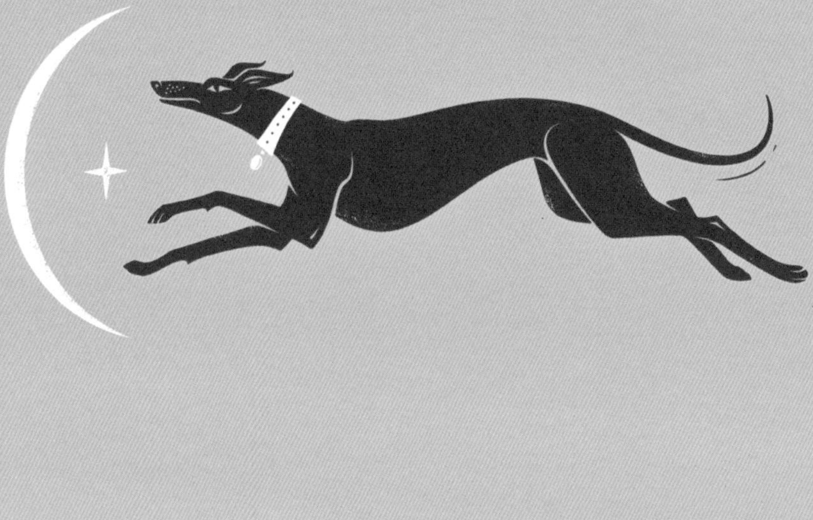

THE
DOG
YEAR

DOGS, MAGIC,
NATURE
AND SPELLS

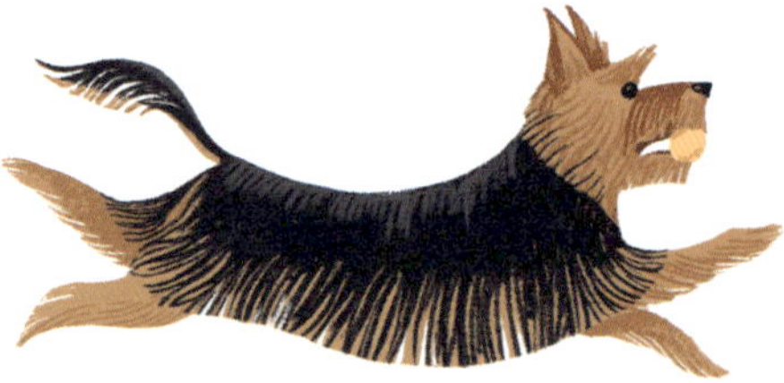

THE DOG YEAR

DOGS, MAGIC,
NATURE
AND SPELLS

ALISON DAVIES

Illustrated by
Anastasia Stefurak

Quadrille

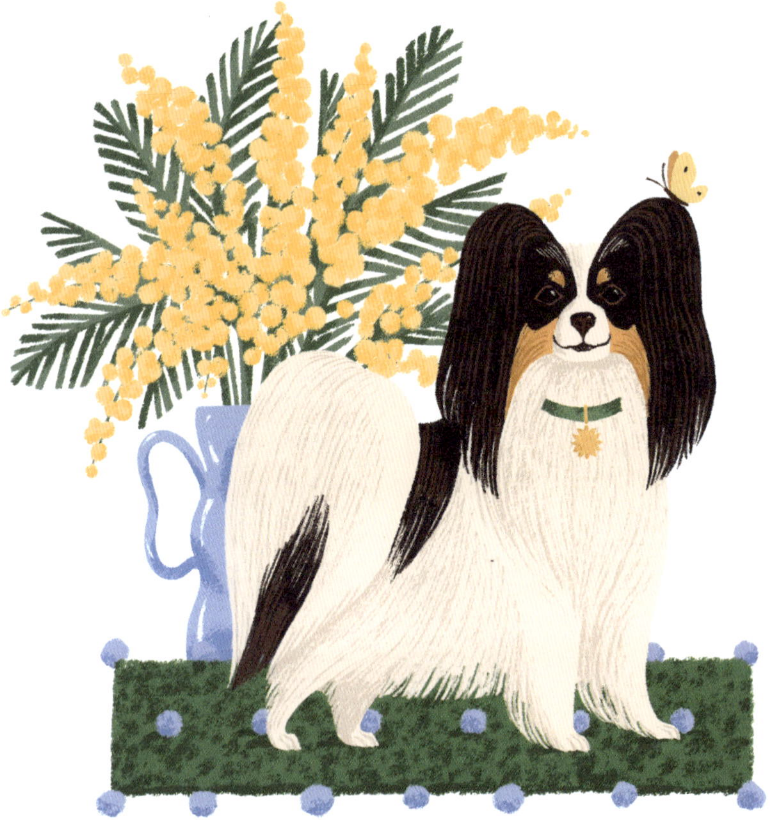

CONTENTS

Introduction 6

JANUARY 10

FEBRUARY 20

MARCH 32

APRIL 42

MAY 52

JUNE 64

JULY 74

AUGUST 84

SEPTEMBER 96

OCTOBER 106

NOVEMBER 116

DECEMBER 128

Mystical Terms Glossary 138
Dog Glossary 140

INTRODUCTION

WELCOME

Dogs bring out the best in us. They encompass every good feature that we as humans aspire to. Their loyal devotion is unquestionable and their enthusiasm for life, and for each precious of moment of the day, is an inspiration. Their 'yes, yes, yes' attitude cannot be matched, as they willingly throw themselves into anything if it means there's fun, discovery and perhaps an errant sausage to be had. Dogs don't do things by halves, as any owner will tell you. They're all in, and that includes their adoration of us. It's fair to say we are pretty loved up when it comes to all things pup. After all, they've been with us since the very beginning in one form or another.

The first wolves may have seemed feral to early humans, but both species soon understood that a kinship of kind could be had. With a little give and take, the humans shared their scraps, the wild dog ancestors helped them hunt, and in time, the two shared hearth and home. The canine began to adapt and to see that teamwork made the dream work, and their eagerness to please was rewarded with full bellies and warm bodies to sleep against. And so the enduring friendship between human and dog was born.

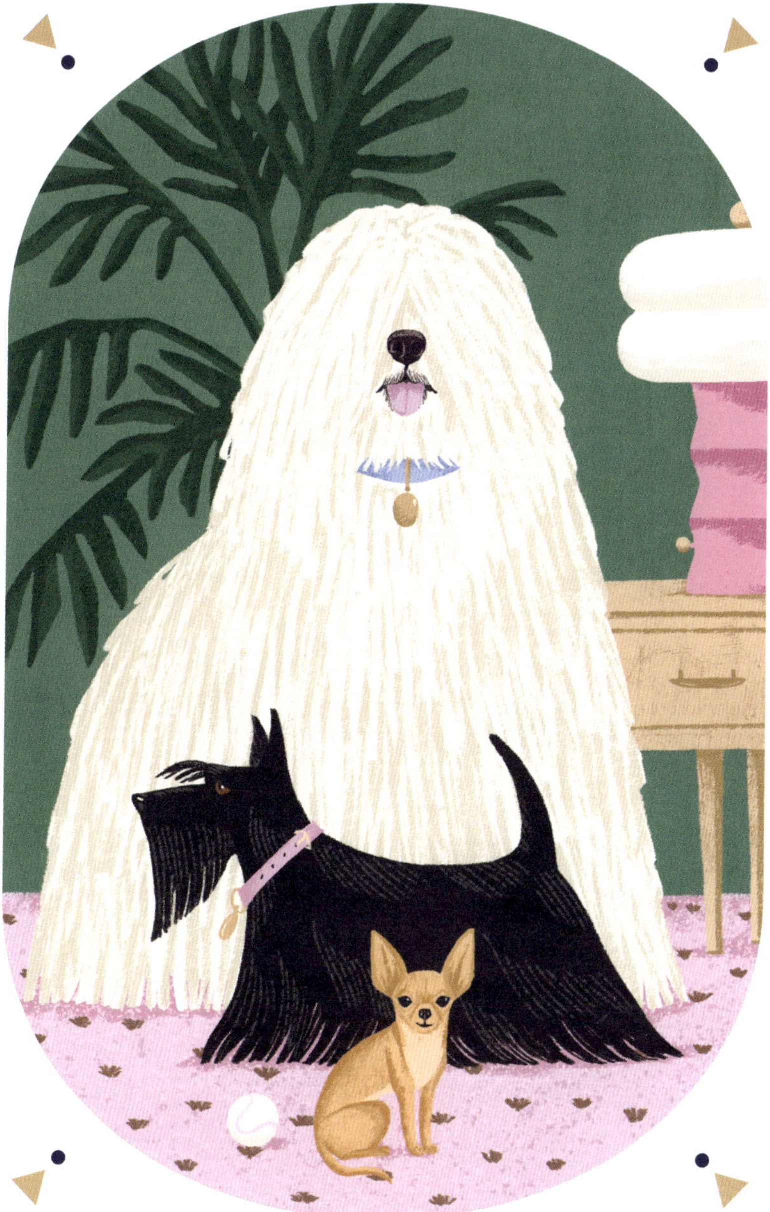

INTRODUCTION

Canines' unfailing loyalty became their superpower, and dogs were soon seen as spiritual guardians, lifelong companions and, if stories are to be believed, guides into the abyss of the otherworld. Dogs were deified and considered gods of the dead and dying, for what other creature could be trusted with such an important role? In canines, humans had found unconditional love and protection, and so each culture created their own version of the dog in god-like form.

To the ancient Egyptians, the dog was Anubis, the revered jackal-headed deity and caretaker of the souls of the recently deceased. He was a dedicated caregiver, embalming and mummifying the dead and escorting their souls onto the afterlife. To the ancient Greeks, the dog was Cerberus, the three-headed dog-like entity that guarded the gates of the Underworld. He was a fearsome beast, valued for his ability to protect the borders between the worlds. The Mesopotamians had Bau, the beautiful dog goddess associated with healing and oaths of honour. The list goes on, but one thing that remains true in every culture: canines, though sometimes mighty and monstrous, were always represented as honourable and devoted in their plight.

INTRODUCTION

This book takes you on a journey looking at some of the mystical representations of the dog from around the world. Within these pages you'll get a glimpse of the myths, legends and quirkier superstitions associated with our clever canines. The seasonal introductions highlight the highs and lows of nature's transitions and how you can help your pup navigate them, while each month showcases a different breed, and looks at the origins of its existence.

You'll learn what makes a dog tick, and the canine lingo that your pup wants you to master. You'll also discover fascinating facts about your furry friends and fun exercises to bring out your playful side within each month. Meanwhile, the joy and magic of the pooch is captured in a monthly spell to help your pup live its best life.

Whether you're a dog owner or lover, or just fascinated by animal myths and legends, this book contains everything you need to celebrate all things canine. So what are you waiting for? Make like a pup and delve into *The Dog Year* for a deeper understanding of these captivating creatures.

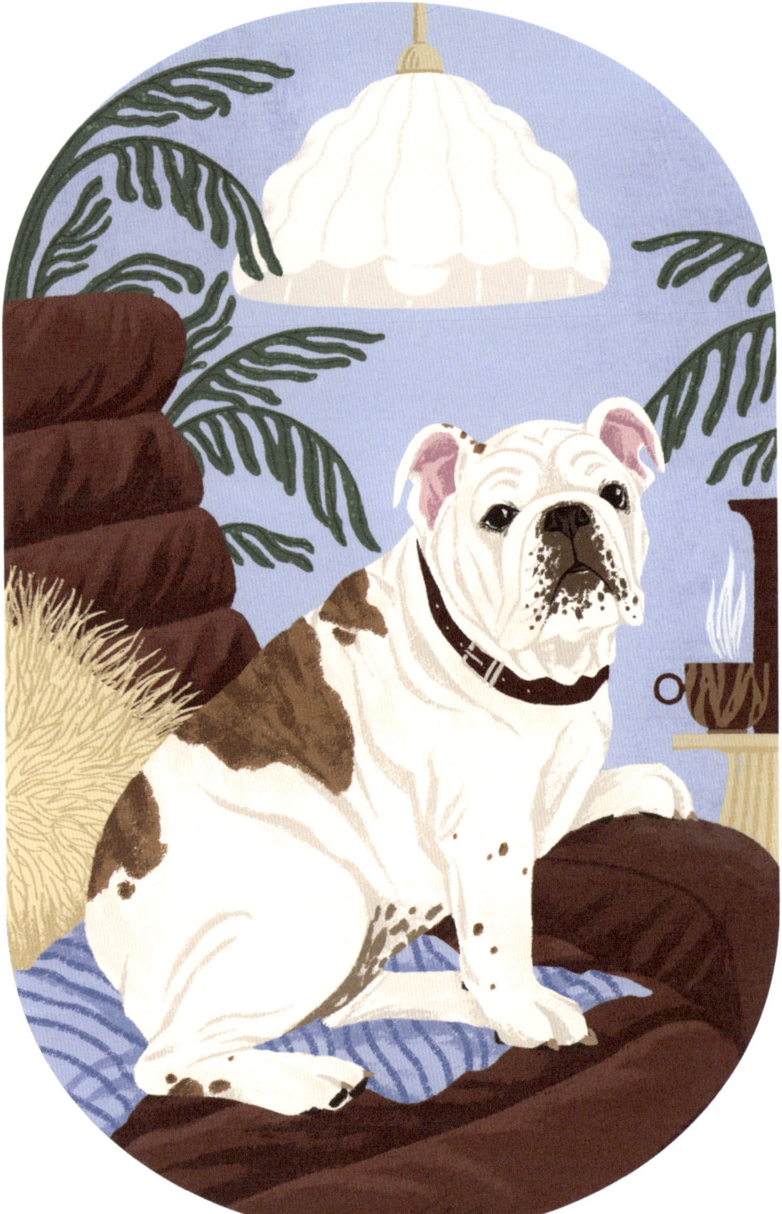

JANUARY

JANUARY

DOG OF THE MONTH

BULLDOG

It's hard to believe that this peace-loving, often lazy pooch was once a ferocious fighter, but the modern-day Bulldog evolved from a breed created thousands of years ago in England as a bull-baiting dog. With a stocky body and powerful legs, the original Bulldog had all the makings of a feisty aggressor, and could hold its own when challenged, although it was thought to be lacking in the brains department.

Historical records from ancient Rome claim that both British and Greek soldiers fought alongside dogs, some of these being the *Pugnaces Britanniae*, a flat-faced broad-mouthed breed, similar in look and build to the Bulldog. It's thought that these are the true ancestors of this canine, but they have also been linked to the Alaunt, a mastiff-like breed with connections to both modern-day Bulldogs and Mastiffs.

While the Bulldog of today is quite a different character compared to the past, and known for its docile and friendly temperament, this sturdy pooch can still be wilful – a remnant of the courageous spirit it displayed when going into battle alongside its human companion. Needing little exercise, this pup enjoys lots of naps and short, but energetic, play sessions, which help to wile away the hours in between snoozing.

JANUARY

DOG SUPERSTITION
THE BLACK DOG

Black dogs get bad press around the world, but especially in European folklore, where they are considered the hounds of Hell. This strange superstition started as a way to explain the disappearance of people from the streets in the dead of night. It was thought that they had been claimed by the Devil, and whisked away by one of his many black hounds.

As the theory progressed and people caught on to this idea, it became a common belief that those who were followed by a black dog had been marked by Satan. As such, it was wise to make sure you were safely home by the witching hour. Some even claimed that the black dogs were witches in disguise looking for mischief.

CLEVER DOG
SNOOT SENSES

Your dog's nose knows everything. With a sense of smell infinitely better than any human, it has the ability to pick up on subtle changes within your personality and how you're feeling. With just one sniff, it can sense when you are stressed out or scared based off the chemicals present in your breath and sweat. Much of this is to do with the way dogs smell. Using both nostrils separately, around 12 to 13 per cent of the air they inhale goes directly to the olfactory epithelium, a thin membranous layer in the nasal cavity that helps to identify odours. While canines can sniff out trouble and disease at the drop of a hat, this ability does decrease with age, along with other senses.

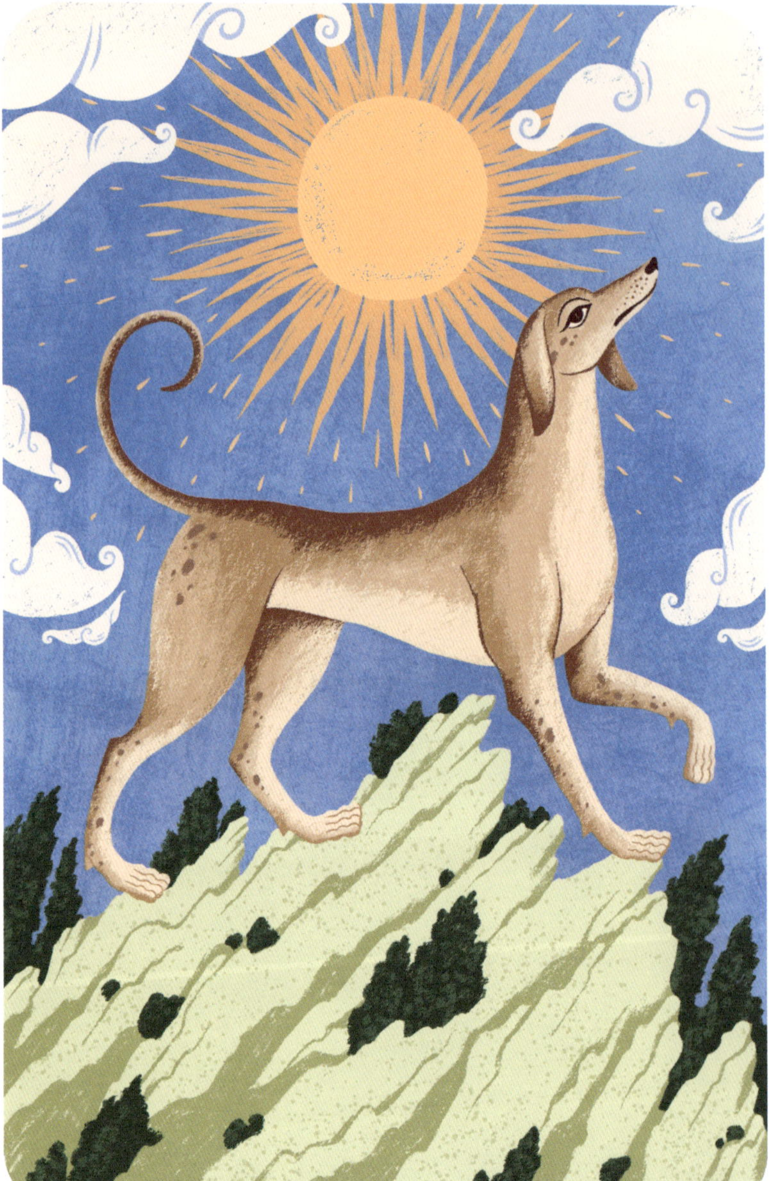

JANUARY

CANINE MYTH

TIHAR AND YUDHISHTHIRA'S DOG

In ancient India, dogs were revered, and in the Hindu faith, they were seen as an emblem of honour and loyalty. Like in most mythologies, dogs were closely linked to death and the passage into the next world, and they were also seen as faithful companions.

In one story, the king Yudhishthira, along with his brothers and the queen, decided to ascend to heaven. This entailed a long and treacherous journey through the Himalayas to reach the very tip of the mountains. During the expedition, a stray dog appeared and took a shine to Yudhishthira, accompanying him through each hardship. As the group got closer to the summit, the journey began to take its toll and the other members died, leaving only Yudhishthira and his trusty hound.

When they eventually reached the peak, the god Indra appeared on a glorious chariot and invited Yudhishthira to ascend to the heavens, but said that entry would be refused to the dog. Yudhishthira, though overjoyed to have reached his goal, would not leave the loyal pup behind. After all, the dog had been with him through every challenge. At this point, the dog transformed into another deity, and praised Yudhishthira for showing such honour and commitment. The king then ascended, and both the dog and Yudhishthira became synonymous with devotion and the bond between humans and canines.

JANUARY

DOG FUN

A GAME OF SOCKS

Cold, rainy days can be tough for your pooch. Keep them entertained and exercised at home with a simple game of tug of war, which stimulates their brain and muscles. You won't need much space, but it's wise to put any breakables away. A couple of old socks tied tightly together make the perfect toy. Remember to let your dog win occasionally, as this makes it more fun for them. When the game is over, get them to drop the socks and reward them with their favourite treat.

JANUARY

PUPPY POWER MOVES

THE TAIL WAG

There's nothing that says 'I love life' more than a wagging tail. You can tell from this one movement when a pooch is happy and present. It's an expression of joy and can reveal just how excited your pup is, based on the speed of the wag. There's something playful about a wiggle, especially when done at speed, and it's a move that you can mimic to boost your own mood, and feel energized.

You will need: music

- To begin, play your favourite dance track. Choose something with a strong beat that makes you want to move.
- Stand with your feet hip width apart, and your shoulders back and relaxed.
- Close your eyes and begin to sway your hips in time with the beat.
- Focus on wiggling your hips and jiggling your tummy in time with the music. Don't think about anything else except the wiggle. Lose yourself in the movement and have fun.
- When the track has finished, relax, give your body a shake and notice how invigorated you feel.

JANUARY

CANINE CHAT

HYPNOTIC EYES

Dogs speak with their eyes, from the lingering stare of a pup watching its owner to the wide-eyed, gleaming gaze of a dog looking for fun. A pooch's peepers reveal their true emotions. They can also show if your dog is feeling threatened. A pup who is trying to avoid confrontation with another canine will look the other way, averting their gaze and often turning their neck so that they cannot see the aggressor. This is a show of submission, and a dog's way of saying, 'I don't want any trouble.' If a pooch appears tense and is staring at another dog, then the opposite is true. Sometimes, a dog will seem disinterested by yawning, nose licking and looking away. Don't be fooled; this pooch is biding its time. Should the situation escalate, it will be ready with a swift reaction.

DOG SPELL

SPELL TO CALM A STRESSED-OUT PUP

The New Year can be a time of change, and even if those transitions are more about you and your life, they can affect your pooch too. If your dog seems restless or nervy, soothe their spirits with this lovely spell, which has a calming effect on both of you.

You will need: lavender essential oil, a small cup half-filled with warm water, a spoon, a lighter or matches, a white candle, your dog's favourite blanket

This spell is best performed on a Monday when you can harness the soothing energy of the moon, or on New Year's Eve when pups are likely to be feeling stressed.

JANUARY

- To begin, find somewhere comfortable to sit, preferably near your dog's bed.
- Add four drops of the lavender essential oil to the cup of water and swirl the contents with the spoon.
- Light the candle (the colour white is soothing) and wrap the blanket around you.
- Close your eyes and take a long deep breath in. As you exhale, imagine all of your worries and fears pouring out from you in that one breath. Continue to breathe in this way to calm your mind.
- When you are ready, gaze into the flame and say, 'I call upon the moon above to soothe my dog with light and love. Let fear be gone and peace remain, as I put out the burning flame.'
- To finish, extinguish the flame and remove the blanket from your shoulder.
- Drizzle a few drops of the scented water over the blanket, then put this on or near your dog's bed.

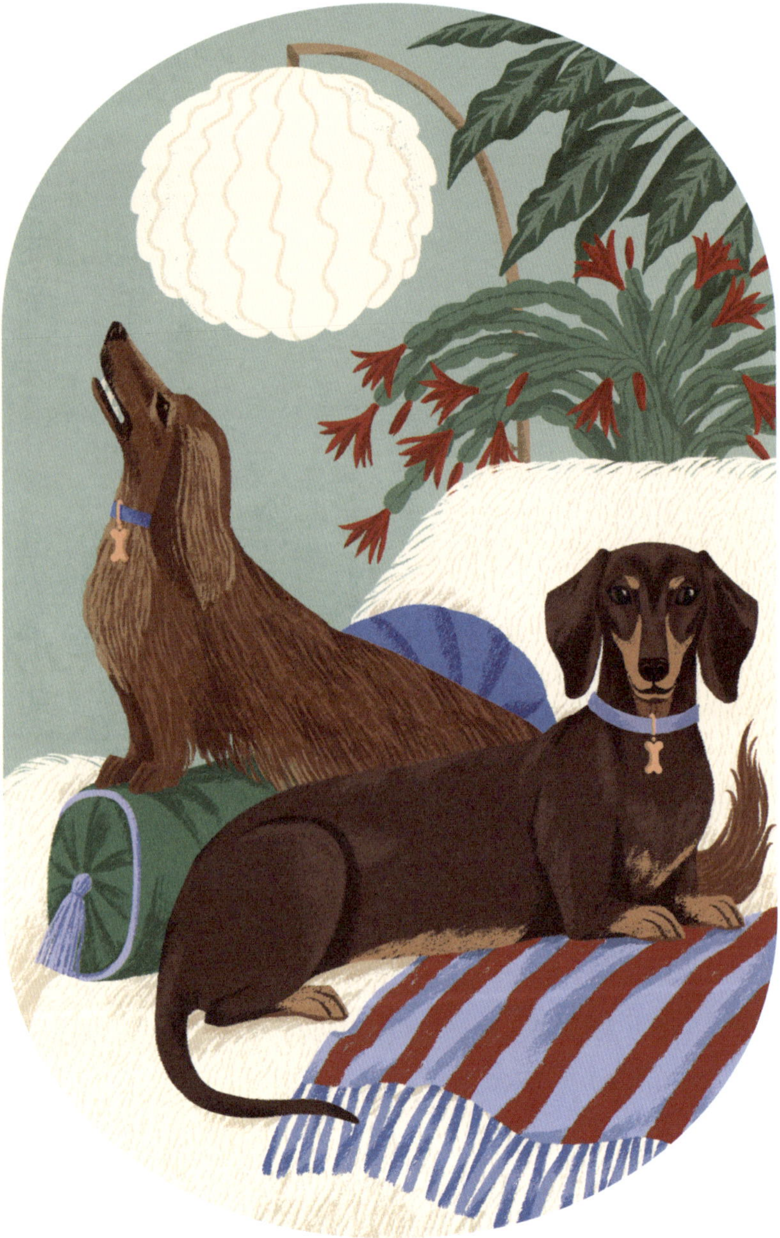

FEBRUARY

FEBRUARY

DOG OF THE MONTH
DACHSHUND

These charming little characters are full of love for their owners, and are often protective, despite their diminutive size. With slender lengthy bodies and short legs they live close to the ground, making them perfect at tracking and hunting small prey such as badgers or rabbits. Originally bred in Germany during the 15th century, their name translates as 'badger hound', although they were also referred to as an 'earth dog' or 'badger creeper'.

The smooth-haired Dachshund was the earliest and most popular variation, being lithe enough to burrow deep into the earth. Their taut sturdy tails made the perfect handle for hunters to pull them free of the dens once the prey had been flushed out. The longer-haired variety, created by crossbreeding with spaniels and terriers to achieve the shaggy look, were equally good hunters and soon matched their shiny, short-haired comrades.

Over time, the Dachshund's primary function as a scent hound became less important, and people grew more enamoured with the breed's affectionate nature and energy. Soon, the pooch took centre stage, winning hearts in the Imperial Court in Germany and even finding favour with Queen Victoria. Today, the Dachshund, or sausage dog as it's often called, makes a playful companion who wants to be at the centre of family life. A great choice if you have children, this little dog needs regular exercise to keep it trim, as it can suffer from back problems thanks to its elongated trunk.

FEBRUARY

DOG SUPERSTITION

SENSITIVE SNOUTS

Dogs are exceptionally loyal to their family, so it's no surprise that they might also be the first to sense when a new member of the tribe is on its way. According to folklore around the world, if a dog lays on the belly of woman who is trying to conceive, she can expect a happy addition, and should a dog become protective and gentle with the woman of the house, then it's likely she could be pregnant. If the dog continues to sniff her tummy during pregnancy, it could be trying to determine the sex of the baby. While this may sound far-fetched, experts say there is some truth to the belief that pooches can predict pregnancy, as their sensitive noses do have the ability to detect hormonal changes.

CLEVER DOG

THE PUPPY PANT

Dogs have a special way of staying cool when the heat is on: they regulate their body temperature by panting. The rapid intake of air works like a humidifier, with each exhalation helping to evaporate excess water from their nose and lungs. This means the cooling happens on the inside, working its way outwards. They also have merocrine glands secreted in their paw pads, which allow them to sweat when they have exerted themselves or on a hot day. The apocrine glands, also situated in their paws, release a pheromone through their sweat, which gives off a scent that is unique to each pooch. Like a fingerprint, this allows other dogs to identify them and pick up their trail easily.

FEBRUARY

CANINE MYTH
RUKUBA

The Bantu people of the African Great Lakes – specifically the Nyanga, a small group based in the Kivu region of the Congo – have always revered the canine, believing it to be man's best friend and also in league with the gods. To them the dog is sacred, and it appears in many of their myths and legends.

One famous story features a Basenji, a small, inquisitive hunting dog often referred to as the 'barkless dog' thanks to its unusually shaped larynx. Unlike other canines, it can only produce a strange yodelling noise. According to Nyanga legend, a Basenji named Rukuba was happily dozing in front of the fire god Nyamurairi's home, oblivious to the approach of the Twa god Nkango (the Twa is a group of indigenous African pygmies, and their stories often overlap with other tribes' mythologies).

Eventually, the dog stirred, alerted by Nkango's footfall, but the Twa god was clever and realized that this friendly creature could help him. And so he made a deal: he promised to look after Rukuba and to be his faithful owner if the dog helped him steal the fire from Nyamurairi. Delighted with this offer, Rukuba assisted Nkango, and so the ancient people of the Kivu region were bestowed the gift of fire.

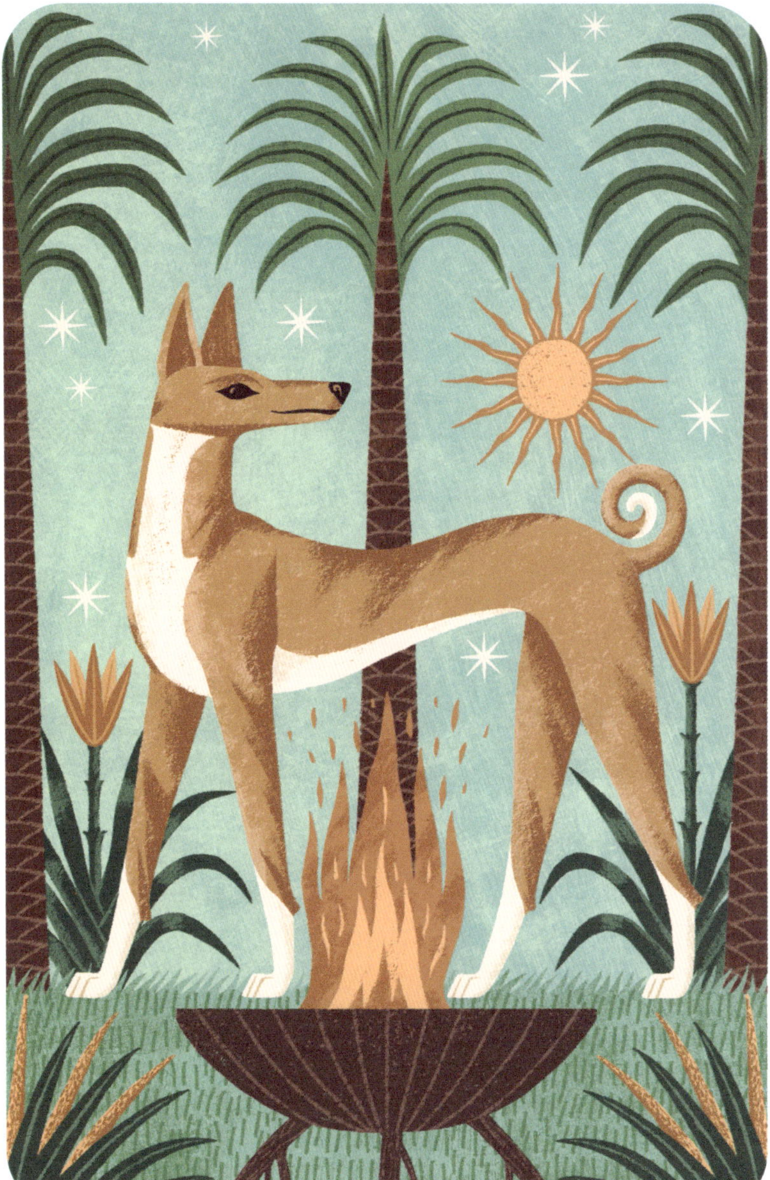

FEBRUARY

CANINE CHAT

TELL TAILS

A dog's tail tells a tale. Like an antenna, it reveals their mood and is one of the key ways they communicate with humans. An upright, high-tailed body wag is like a fist pump. It's your dog's way of saying, 'Hey, isn't life great? I'm so happy!' It can also reveal when they're excited to see you. If their tail is slightly curved, it could indicate some tension or that they're super-alert and looking for action. A low, slow wag suggests your pooch is upset or cautious, which can happen from time to time. But if it continues, get your dog a health check, as they might not be feeling their best. If their tail is positioned close to the ground but relaxed, then they're calm and comfortable, but a dog whose tail is low and between their legs may feel threatened or anxious.

PUPPY POWER MOVES
SENSORY SNIFF

Dogs sniff a lot because it helps them make sense of their environment. They take in the air so that they can identify scents and understand where they are, and what is going on. Follow suit with this breathing exercise, which engages the senses and helps to promote clarity.

- Close your mouth and draw a long deep breath in through your nose.
- Hold the breath in your chest for the count of four, and then slowly release it, letting it filter out between your lips.
- Take another breath in and hold the breath for the count of five, before releasing it again.
- Continue to breath in this way and notice what you smell and how fresh and cool the air is. Notice too how it tastes upon your tongue.
- Repeat for three minutes, and if your mind wanders, bring it back to the breathing and your senses.

FEBRUARY

DOG FUN

TREASURE HUNT

Dogs need regular exercise to keep them in tip-top condition, but they also need an active brain to feel their best. There's nothing your pup loves more than interacting with you, so games that stimulate their natural hunting instinct will keep them on their toes, and provide hours of fun for you both.

A treasure hunt is one the easiest games to play with your dog, and it doesn't require a lot planning. To begin, take a treat, and let them watch as you hide it somewhere obvious. Then let them find it. Once they get the idea of the game and they've had some success, you can turn up the difficulty by hiding the treat in a different room. If you have any empty boxes, arrange them in a pattern on the floor and hide the treat inside one of them, then watch as your dog goes in search of its reward.

DOG SPELL

SPELL TO LIFT YOUR POOCH'S MOOD

Dogs aren't just pets, they're a part of the family, so when they're under the weather, everyone feels it. If it's a physical problem you can take them to vets, but sometimes it's emotional and about putting the pep back in their step. This easy ritual should help to lift their mood.

You will need: a piece of citrine, your dog's favourite toy

This spell is best performed around midday on a Sunday so that you can tap into the power of the sun.

- Find a window ledge and position the toy and the citrine (a crystal known for its joyful energy) next to one another so that the toy can soak up the crystal's uplifting energy, and the vibrancy of the sun. It doesn't matter if it's not a sunny day; the sun will still be present and at the height of its power. Leave for around 5–10 minutes.

- Stand or sit close by and take a few deep breaths to clear and calm your mind.

- When you're ready, close your eyes and picture the sun shining brightly above your pooch as it sleeps. Imagine your dog bathed in the golden sunlight. For every breath you take, turn up the strength of that light and see it shimmering even brighter.

- Spend a few minutes sending love to your pup, then open your eyes.

- Remove the citrine and keep it somewhere safe.

- Take the toy and put it in your dog's bed.

SPRING

Winter's harsh mask begins to crack with the appearance of spring. Full of freshness, spring brings a feast of fragrance for our four-legged friends to enjoy. Buds burst through the ground along with an abundance of early blooms. These flowers, often vibrant and powerfully scented, are a delight to any curious canine nose. Tiny mammals that spent the winter months tucked away now stir, pushing up through layers of soil and adding their own distinct aroma to the sensory palette. The trees and plants begin to regain their original zest, peppering pollen upon the breeze. Mother Earth is rousing her troops.

Your dog will experience an awakening of sorts as its senses are triggered by the plethora of sights, sounds and smells. There's no time for paws to pause; indeed, your pooch may seem somewhat restless, eager to explore this changing environment. This kind of spring fever is perfectly natural, and any wilful behaviour can be tempered with some active training sessions and plenty of exercise. You may also notice a change in their coat as they shed any excess hair ready for the warmer months. It's time to lift the layers, shake the weight of winter from those sleepy bones and step out with renewed vigour.

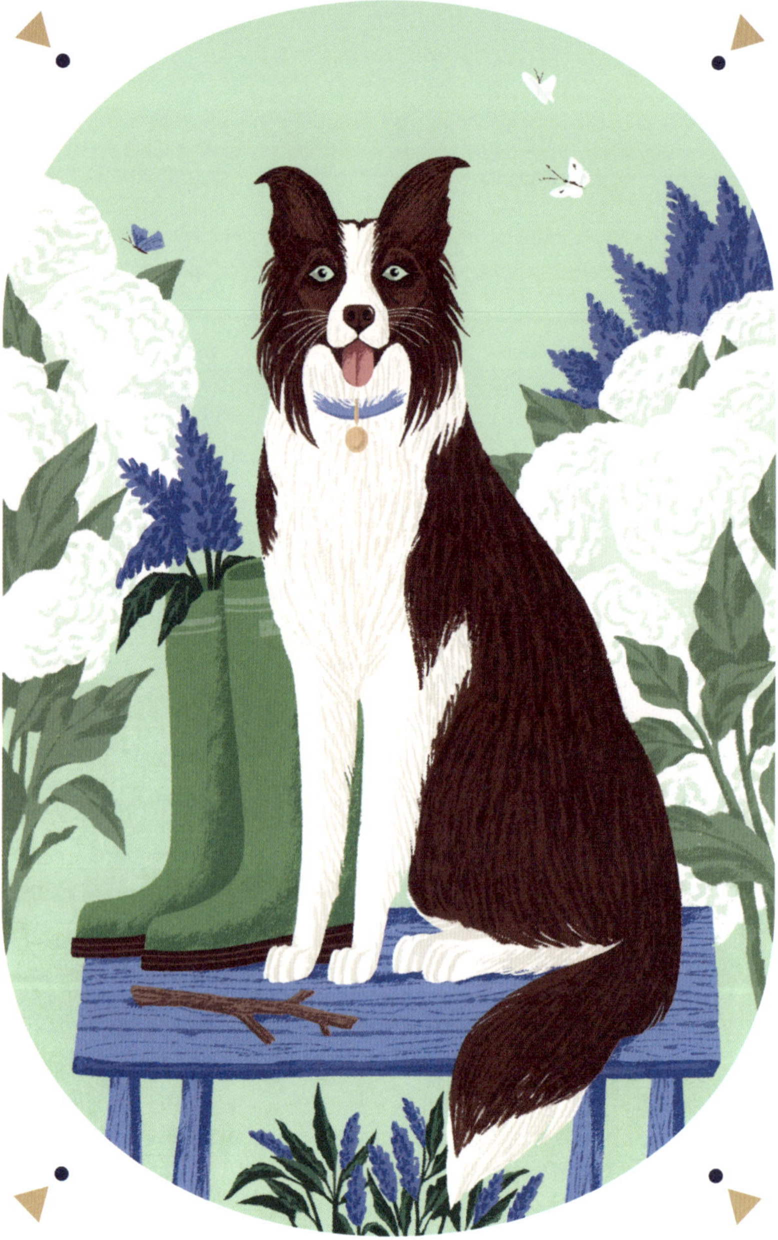

MARCH

MARCH

DOG OF THE MONTH
BORDER COLLIE

This engaging pup is a descendant of a line of landrace Collies originally found on the British Isles. Bred to work, the Border Collie's drive to steer anything that moves, and its enthusiasm to please, make it a favourite choice among farmers and families.

Whether it's herding sheep or children, this dog is diligent and dedicated in its approach. Its Collie moniker has its roots in the Anglo-Scottish word colley, which means 'black' and appeared towards the end of the 19th century. Before that, it also appeared as the Celtic word for 'useful', a fitting accolade for such a willing worker.

Strong and muscular, the Border Collie has an athletic build, which allows it to navigate the landscape and run at speed. Highly intelligent, this is one pooch that rarely lacks energy and is likely to keep any owner on their toes. Don't be put off by the infamous Border Collie stare, also known as 'giving the eye'. This can appear intimidating at first glance, but it's a predatory behaviour inherited from their wolf ancestors, and it has a purpose. This intense gaze is the Border Collie's primary tool for keeping errant sheep in check.

Loving and loyal, this pooch will go the extra mile for its family, human or otherwise. One famous tale from 1923 features a Collie named Bobbie the Wonder Dog, who was separated from his family after being attacked by a pack of dogs. Despite this, Bobbie travelled 2,551 miles to be reunited with them, a feat that took him six arduous months to complete.

DOG SUPERSTITION

LUCKY PAWS

Dogs, like most animals, seem to be good judges of character. It's no surprise then that there are superstitions that suggest if a strange dog takes a liking to you for no apparent reason, you are blessed. Around the world, it's commonly believed that if a stray follows you home, it's a sign of good luck, and should it step inside your abode, then expect an abundance of good fortune.

Dogs have a talent for sniffing out treasure and spotted dogs come out on top when it comes to luck. Should you meet a Dalmatian on the way to a business meeting, expect a positive outcome. Greyhounds are also beneficial, especially if they have a white spot anywhere upon their body. Pure white dogs are associated with wealth and it's thought that if you see three such dogs in a row, you can expect a hefty windfall.

MARCH

CANINE MYTH
CÙ-SÌTH

Should you dare to explore the highlands of Scotland and wander the moors, you might encounter the spectral hound known as Cù-Sìth. A giant beast the size of a bull, with shaggy, mossy green hair that hangs about its ghostly form, this dog will fix you with its fiery eyes. Once it has you in its sights, be warned: if it starts to howl, then your soul is marked for the otherworld. Whether that's the afterlife or the fairy realm, no one knows. If it howls three times, it's a portend of doom, so it's best to seek refuge inside before the third wail to stand a chance of survival.

According to Scottish folklore, the Cù-Sìth is a fairy dog, which would explain the colour of its fur, as green is commonly associated with the fey. With large paws the size of hands and a braided tail, the Cù-Sìth has the ability to slip between worlds, often appearing out of thin air. This ethereal being is hard to avoid and even turns up in Irish myth as Cú Sidhe. This dog inhabits the rugged landscape, living between rocks and crevices and preys upon hapless strangers. In particular, the beast has a penchant for young mothers, stealing them away to the fairy otherworld to nurse fairy children.

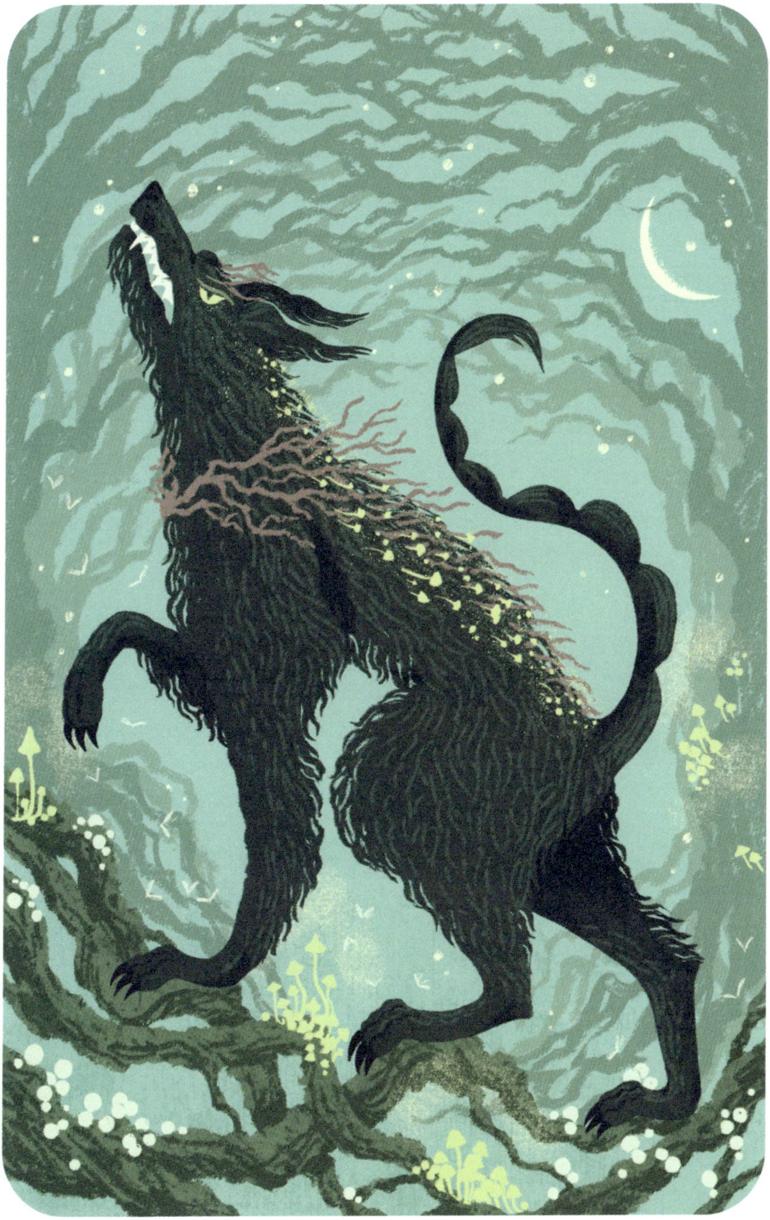

THE DOG'S DINNER
SWIFT AND SPEEDY

Dogs are built to run, and some of the larger, more athletic types are super speedy. The Greyhound, for example, is a lean, mean sprinting machine, able to launch into a run within seconds of standing, and reach up to 45 miles per hour. This fleet and nimble hound is more than a match for the cheetah, for while the big cat can reach a running speed of around 75 miles per hour, it can only maintain this magnificent feat for around 30 seconds. The Greyhound has the ability to run at a nifty 35 miles per hour for at least seven miles, making its commitment to speed second to none. Even if your pooch isn't a fan of racing around, it's important to give them the opportunity to run, as regular exercise maintains their body health, strength and mental wellbeing.

CANINE CHAT
BELLY RUBS

When a dog feels good, it shows in their posture. A calm, confident pooch will stand on all fours with a relaxed frame. It's likely that their mouth will be open and their tongue may be out. If a dog is in a playful mood, then you'll see it bow down slightly by crouching lower to the ground with the front half of their body. Their tail may be up and wagging to match the vibe, and their mouth will be open. This pup is in game mode and inviting you to join in the fun!

When a dog is full of joy and feeling particularly trusting, it will lay on its back with its belly exposed for a rub. This shows that the pooch is super-relaxed in your company and doesn't feel threatened by exposing itself.

PUPPY POWER MOVES

THE LIVELY LEAP

Whether they're chasing you, each other or having bouncy fun with their favourite ball, dogs know the importance of being playful. Breaking free and letting go is good for the soul, so follow suit with some lively skipping moves that will put a spring in your step.

You will need: a skipping rope (optional)

- Start by counting four beats in your head. Keep repeating, and every time you reach the fourth beat, take a gentle leap in the air, then increase the speed of your counting. If you have a skipping rope, you can use that, otherwise jump on the spot. All you need to do is carefully time your jumps and build up speed and height.

- Be creative, and if you're not using a skipping rope, throw your arms in the air, or pull a shape as you spring. Embrace your inner pup and have fun with this.

- Continue to jump or skip for a couple of minutes, then slowly reduce the speed and come to a stop.

- Breathe deeply and give your body a shake.

MARCH

DOG FUN

A LOT OF WOOF

According to research, the average dog can learn at least 165 words. That's a fair bit of language. If you're already training your dog, it's likely they'll know simple commands like 'stay' and 'sit', but you can improve their knowledge and boost their IQ by playing the name game. The simplest way to do this is to name their favourite toy. For example, if it's a felt bear, you might call it Teddy. Every time you pick it up or pass it to your dog, repeat the name, and keep repeating it until the pooch gets used to it. Eventually you'll be able to ask them to 'Go find Teddy' and they will be able to understand.

DOG SPELL

SPELL TO BOOST YOUR PUP'S CONFIDENCE WITH OTHER DOGS

Dogs, like humans, come in all shapes and sizes and have very different personalities. Some pooches love to mingle, and others prefer the peace and quiet of home. But if your pup is particularly shy and nervous around other dogs, this spell might help.

You will need: a picture of a wolf, your dog's lead, a piece of amber

This spell is best performed on a Tuesday, which is governed by Mars, the assertive and confident Roman god whose influence can inspire courage.

- Sit with the picture of the wolf in front of you and place your dog's lead in a circle over the top of the image.

- Place the piece of amber (a crystal associated with courage, confidence and positive energy) in the centre of this arrangement.

- Spend a few minutes looking at the wolf picture, and think about the qualities that this creature represents. The wolf is unafraid to go it alone, but is also a tribe animal. It has the strength needed to find its place within the pack, and to feel secure with the other members. Your pup is a descendant of the wolf, and can harness the same power.

- Take a deep breath and say, 'May the power of the wolf and the strength it represents imbue my furry friend with greater confidence.'

- Leave the lead with the picture and the amber together until your next walk, and repeat the spell two or three times for the next week to see results.

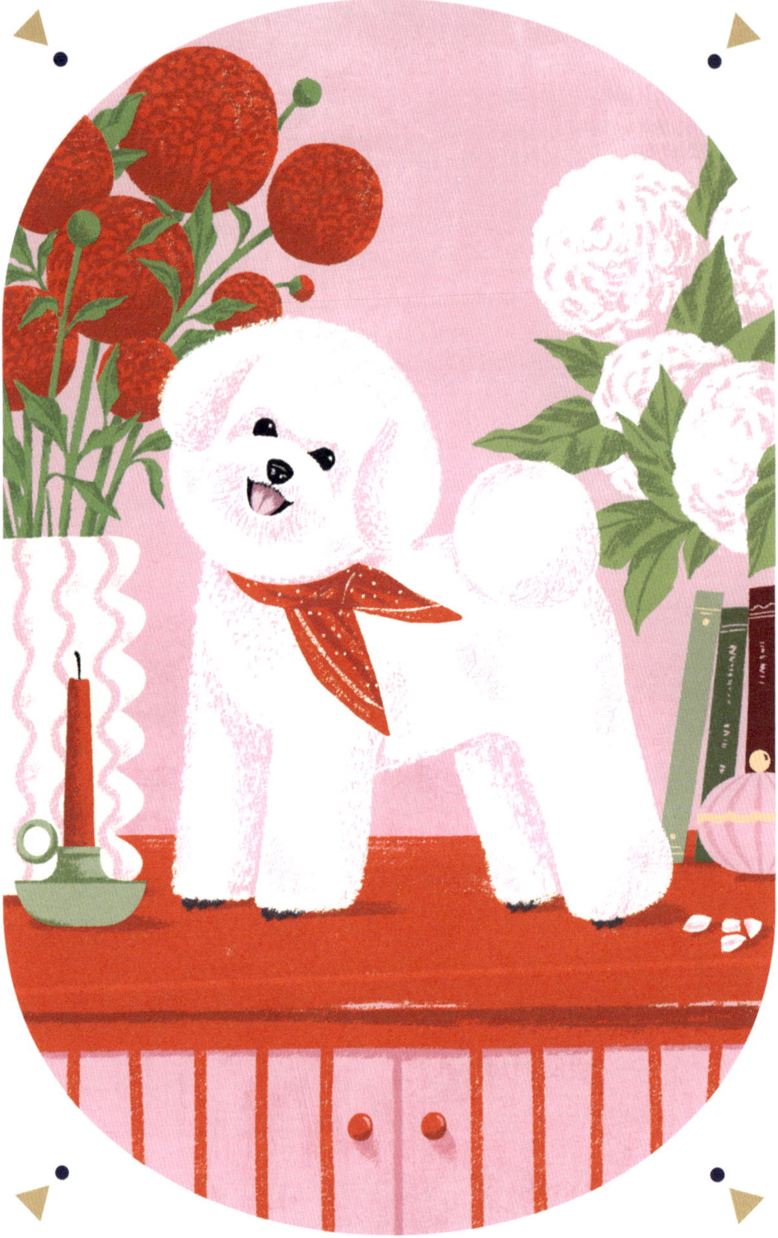

APRIL

APRIL

DOG OF THE MONTH

BICHON FRISÉ

Their name may be French, meaning 'fluffy dog', but this cute and friendly pooch is a descendant of the water Spaniel and finds its origins in the Canary Islands. Some historians believe these dogs were brought to France by travellers, while others claim that Italian traders carried the breed to mainland Europe. Whoever was responsible, the fact remains that this bubbly little pup was highly esteemed and treasured by nobility, who saw the Bichon Frisé as a status symbol. King Henry III was a huge fan, having several over the years, and it's believed he carried one in a small basket hung around his neck.

With it's fluffy Poodle-like coat and playful temperament, it's easy to see why this dog was such a hit. Add to that the traditional white coat and shining black eyes, and you have an award-worthy pooch. Proudly pampered by their owners, the French nobility lavished so much attention on these pups that they invented the verb 'bichonner', meaning 'to pamper', to describe their daily adorations. This soon became a part of the everyday language. Highly intelligent, this breed is easy to train and enjoys plenty of cuddle time with its human tribe, but can become anxious and depressed, if left alone for long stretches.

DOG SUPERSTITION

GHOST-SPOTTING DOGS

It's no surprise that dogs have a sixth sense when you consider their association with death and the afterlife in mythologies around the world. In Persia, the dog is considered a guardian of the soul, and is often placed by the bed of someone who is sick or dying to keep evil spirits at bay. If the person passes over, the dog then escorts them on to the afterlife.

The Aztec god Xolotl was thought to have the head of a dog on a human body. His role was protective, and he would guide lost souls to the Underworld. In the Middle Ages in Europe, dogs were considered spiritual beings who could predict death. They lurked in the shadows ready to steal errant souls and carry them on to the next life. According to popular superstition, when a pooch stares into the distance or at any empty space, it's likely there's a spirit hovering.

CANINE MYTH

THE CADEJO

According to the indigenous tribes of Central America, should you roam the streets at night, you'll likely encounter a spirit dog called a Cadejo. Depending on your luck, it could help or hinder your journey, for there are two versions of this particular ghoul. The black one, often considered the Devil incarnate, will trick you and lead you to your doom, while the white version will provide safe passage and guide you to your destination.

That said, the motivation of either often changes depending on the country you are in. Both versions have pale blue eyes when calm, but should they get angry, these will turn a blazing red hue. As big as a bull with goat-like hooves, the Cadejo is not a beast to be ignored. Should you turn away from its glare or try and talk to it, you'll be sent mad.

It's thought that the white Cadejo has a soft spot for drunks and homeless wanderers, protecting them against the creatures of the night, while the black version will lure them into the woods and encourage them to make bad decisions. This good versus evil narrative was reworked by Spanish conquistadors who came to Central America. Being heavily influenced by Christianity but also believers of the supernatural, they combined the two schools of thought to create a powerful legend that has stood the test of time.

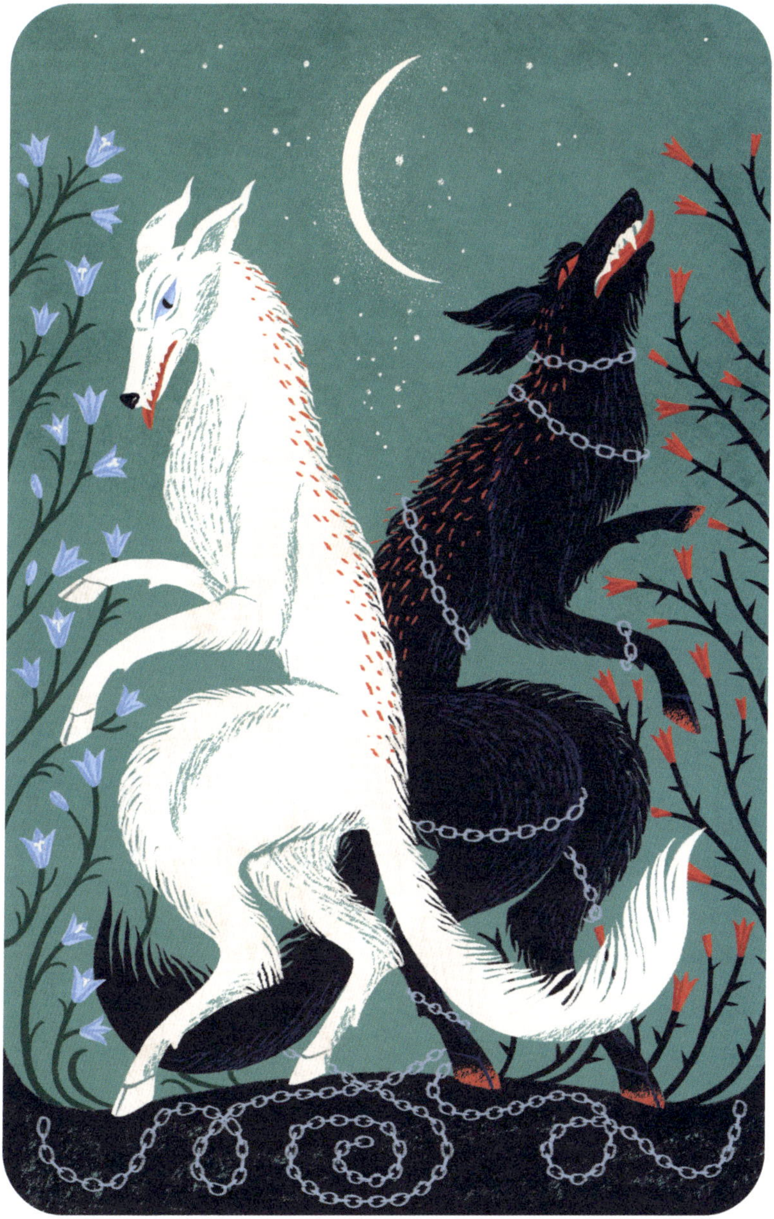

APRIL

DOG FUN

THE OBSTACLE CHALLENGE

Agility is a key component of your dog's health and wellbeing, as regular movement promotes joint flexibility, tones muscles and gets rid of excess fat. Taking them for walks will help with this, but there are also things you can do in the home and garden to keep them in tip-top shape.

If the weather is bad, create an obstacle course in your living room using old cushions of different sizes, cardboard boxes and toys. Encourage your dog to step over and around the various obstacles by offering them a treat. Once they complete the course, give them their reward, then repeat the process, building up speed. You can do a similar thing in your garden using chairs, tables and cushions.

CANINE CHAT

LOVE LANGUAGE

A dog's bark is full of nuances. It can reveal a range of emotions from excitement and joy, to fear and loneliness. A low guttural bark suggests your pooch is not happy and could be feeling threatened or protective, depending on the situation. If their bark is higher pitched and more of yelp, then you have a very excited pup on your hands. This type of bark is your dog's way of saying, 'Hello, I'm happy you're here!' A high-pitched bark is also a sign that a pup is feeling lonely and wants to engage. The number of barks is also important: if it's a series of barks then a dog is more aroused, whereas a single sound is a bit like a question mark, and often used when a pooch is trying to make sense of things.

APRIL

PUPPY POWER MOVES

PUPPY POSE

Dogs can pull a range of poses depending on how they feel. This pose is super-relaxed, while extending the spine and opening the chest. It's perfect for those days when you feel tense and need a quick stretch to centre yourself.

You will need: a yoga mat

- Get on all fours on the mat, with your knees directly beneath your hips and your hands flat and beneath your shoulders.
- Take a deep breath in and slowly slide forwards, bringing your chest towards the floor and sliding your arms out in front of you at the same time. Imagine you are melting into the ground, but keep your bottom raised and your hips over your knees.
- Exhale and hold this position for five seconds.

APRIL

THE DOG'S DINNER
HUNGRY HOUNDS

Dogs have many senses that excel our own, but there is one that doesn't meet the grade: their sense of taste. With only 1,700 tastebuds, as opposed to humans who have approximately 9,000, it's easy to see why anything goes when it comes to a quick snack. This lack of discrimination is something they've inherited from their wolf ancestors, who would often gorge on grass to satisfy their hunger, and also to expel anything suspicious they might have eaten. Pooches today have less need to scavenge food, but will still eat just about anything, including glass and faeces. This is partly down to their curious nature, something established at a young age, and their lack of tastebuds. Whether it's a prime steak from next door's barbeque or their own poop, it matters little to a hungry hound.

APRIL

DOG SPELL

SPELL TO STRENGTHEN THE BOND BETWEEN YOU AND YOUR DOG

Dogs love to be loved. Their natural instinct is to make us feel better. It doesn't take long for a pooch to become a treasured part of the family, but if your dog is a rescue or it hasn't had the best start in life, it can take time for the bond to form. To strengthen these ties, try this simple spell.

You will need: a piece of rose quartz

This spell is best performed on a Friday, which is governed by the planet of love, Venus.

- Wait for a moment when your dog is feeling relaxed, for example, when they're having a snooze or they've settled down in their bed.
- If you can get close without causing a disturbance, sit near them. Otherwise, you can sit at a distance, as long as you can see them.
- Hold the rose quartz (associated with loving energy) in both hands.
- As you breathe in, imagine the lovely pink energy of the stone flowing into your body.
- As you exhale, imagine that loving energy pouring out from your heart in a stream of rosy light. Picture it flowing into your dog and enveloping them in love. Continue to visualize this as you breathe for a few minutes.
- In your mind, send your pooch a wish for love and tell them how much they mean to you. Release all of that affection in your outwards breath. Then, relax and let them soak up all the loving energy that you have sent.

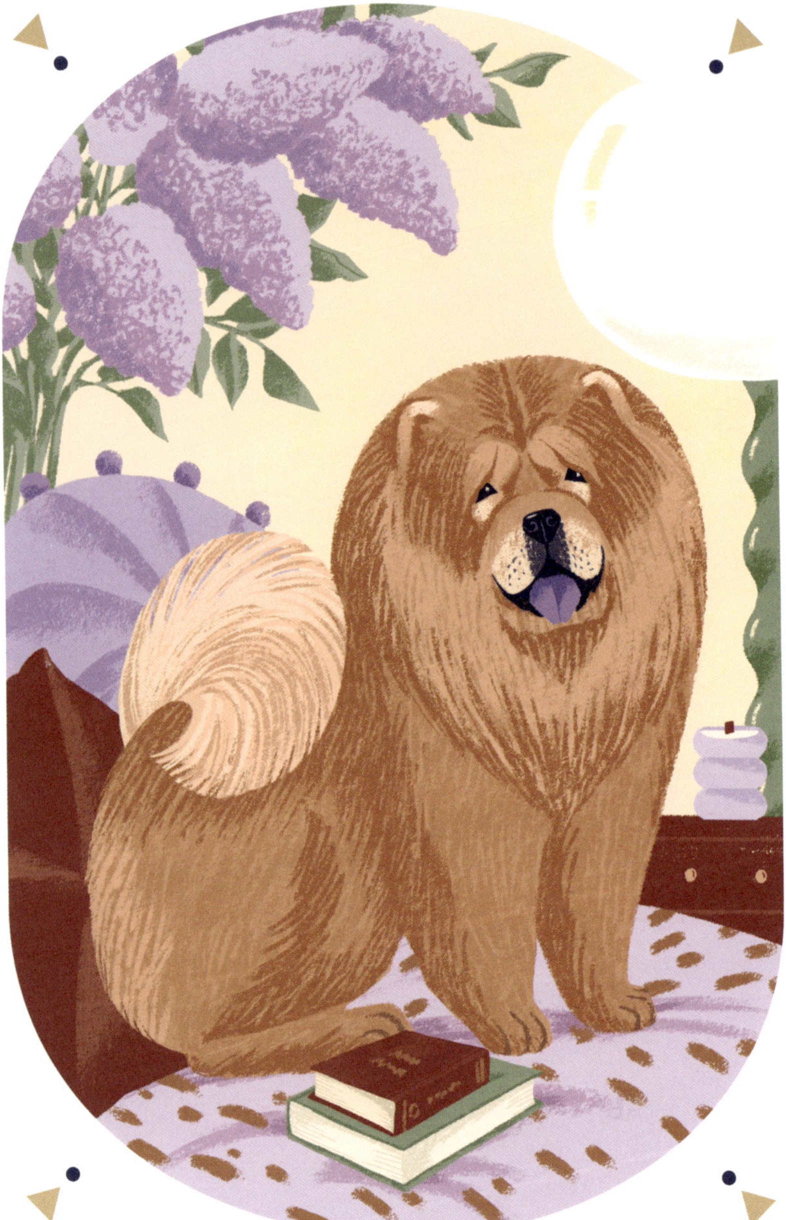

MAY

MAY

DOG OF THE MONTH
CHOW CHOW

This bear-like beauty is an ancient breed originating in East Asia. It appears on Chinese artefacts as far back as 206 BCE. With its sturdy stature, thick neck and dense layers of fur, the Chow Chow is a hardy pooch, which goes some way to explain why stone statues of the breed are often used as sentinels keeping watch at Buddhist temples.

The Chow Chow has a list of distinguishing features including an extra pair of teeth, making it unlike any other dog breed. By far the most distinctive facet is its blue-black tongue, which can also look purple in certain lights. There are many tales in folklore that attempt to explain the significance of their tongue, and how the breed acquired this strange attribute. One myth claims that, at the beginning of time, the Chow Chow, which resembled a dragon, hated the night so much that it stretched up into the sky and licked away the darkness. From that moment on, the day was born, and the dog was gifted with its uniquely hued tongue as a punishment from the gods. Another story suggests that the Chow Chow happened to lick up a few drops of the sky as it was being painted. In reality, a genetic mutation that affects the tongue's pigment is the reason for this colour transformation.

DOG SUPERSTITION

HEALING HOUNDS

The early Celts were huge fans of dogs, and believed that being near them could rapidly accelerate healing. Some of this belief comes from folklore, and in particular the goddess of healing, Sirona, who was always accompanied by a dog. Many early images of this deity depict her hound licking the wounds of the sick to knit the wounds back together Coupled with the reality that dogs tend to lick their own wounds to help them heal, it's easy to see where the roots of this superstition come from.

During the 18th and 19th century, Pugs were considered to be supremely magical. They had the ability to heal in a number of ways, from relieving headaches and fevers to drawing infections from the human body. It was thought that this little dog would pull the illness into its own tiny body where the illness would be defeated. In reality, the pooch was doing what it does best: being a companion and offering comfort to those in need.

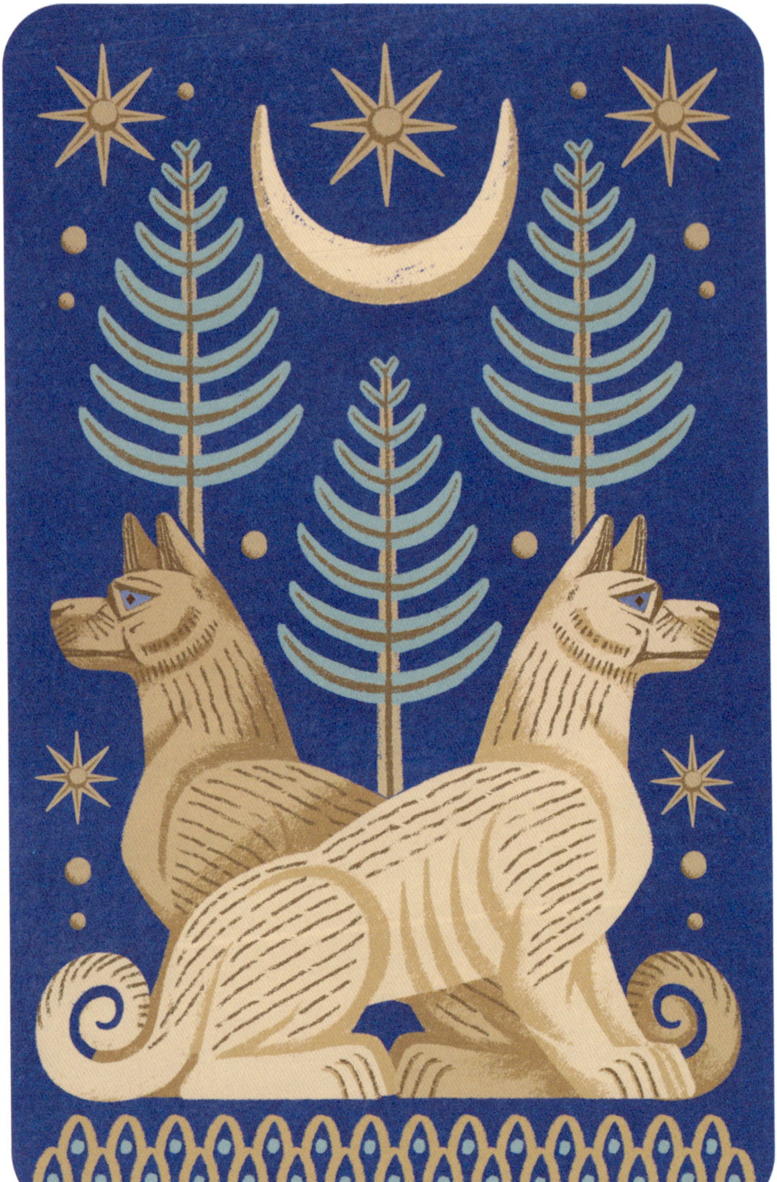

CANINE MYTH

THE DOG CULT OF MESOPOTAMIA

The beautiful goddess Gula, also known as Ninisina, was a Mesopotamian deity, patron of the city of Isin and guardian of dogs. Most commonly recognized for her healing powers, she was also the goddess of medicine, physicians and midwives. All canines were under her protection, and wherever she roamed a pack of dogs would follow. Sometimes the goddess would appear in canine form as a way of showing her devotion to the animal. Those who worshipped her would often craft small clay dogs to leave at her temple as a way of petitioning her help.

The temple in Isin was fittingly named é-ur-gi-ra, which translates as 'dog house', and became a refuge and a place where the cult of Gula could be found. At the time, people would pledge their allegiances to the goddess, and often swear oaths, calling on the sacred dog to assist them. Being the mother of healing, Gula was a powerful deity and therefore her sacred animal, the dog, was also revered. All dogs were allowed to wander freely in and out of the temple, with many buried and entombed within its walls.

CANINE CHAT

EXPRESSIVE EARS

If you want to know how your dog is feeling, pay attention to their ears. Whether they're floppy and big or short and spiky, these cute appendages reveal their truth in the way they're positioned. If a pooch is happy and relaxed, their ears will be in neutral position, sitting easy on their head. Ears pricked up means they've likely heard something that's piqued their interest. If both ears are constantly changing position, then a pup may be confused, especially if they shift their head to one side or the other. A fearful dog will drop and pin their ears back close to their body, but if a dog wants to show they mean no harm, they might also drop their ears slightly but appear relaxed in every other way.

CLEVER DOG

MUCKY PUPS

A dog's toilet habits can seem unconventional when viewed through the eyes of a human, but clever canines have the upper paw. Almost everything they do has a reason or meaning. Interestingly, dogs are highly tuned in to the environment, and in general like to poop in alignment with the earth's magnetic field, which is why it can take them some time to choose the perfect spot. Once they've found a place that fits the bill, they'll probably carry out a series of twirls on the spot. This strange behaviour fulfils a range of needs: it helps them establish a secure footing for what follows, and is also a great way to spread their scent. Being super-vigilant, it allows them to assess the area and get a clear picture of who is around.

PUPPY POWER MOVES

THE WIGGLE STRETCH

If you have a pooch, you'll be no stranger to this manoeuvre. It's all about the joy of the stretch and being playful, and it's something that dogs do with little thought. This exercise helps to work your core and gives your spine and waist a gentle stretch at the same time.

You will need: a yoga mat

- To begin, lay on your back with your arms at either side and your legs raised off the floor, knees bent.
- Press your lower back into the mat and rock your legs and hips gently from side to side. Feel your connection to the floor, and the sensation as the movement massages your lower back muscles.
- Extend your arms outwards at the side, so they're stretched out upon the floor.
- Continue to move from side to side, but put more energy into it. You should feel this working your hips and your core.
- After a minute of this, cease rocking and take a long deep breath in.
- Stretch your legs out and slowly lower them to the floor as you exhale.

MAY

DOG FUN

PUP PAMPERING

Dogs crave attention from their owners and one of the best ways to show them you care is by performing a gentle massage. This is a lovely thing to do for both of you, as it strengthens the bond between you. Wait until your pooch is relaxed and laying on their bed or close to you, and begin with some petting. Then, apply light pressure to your strokes and work your way along their back. Use circular movements with your fingertips and focus on areas such as between the shoulder blades, down the shanks, and towards the rear.

DOG SPELL

SPELL TO FIND A LOST DOG

While it's always best to report a lost dog and go down the usual routes of finding your pet, a little magical assistance can help. A simple spell that tunes in to the bond you share will help to summon your pooch, and bring them home.

You will need: a lighter or matches, a red candle, a picture of your dog, your dog's collar or an old collar

This spell is best performed on a Thursday, which is governed by the planet Jupiter and associated with successful outcomes.

- Light the red candle (red is the colour of action, movement and positive energy) and position it in a window so that it can be seen from the outside.
- Place the picture next to the candle and hold the collar in both hands.
- Stand before the picture and candle, close your eyes and imagine your dog stood in front of you.
- Say their name three times, as if you're calling them towards you.
- Imagine them running to you, and feel the joy and love as they leap into your arms. Know that your dog has heard you calling them.
- Say, 'As I see, please let it be.'
- Let the candle burn down, and leave it next to the picture.

SUMMER

Just as spring settles into its tender dance, there's yet another shift and the wheel of the year turns again. Make way for the heady intoxication of summer. A profusion of brightness sets the earth on fire, turning up the heat and framing the planet in a golden glow. Flowers turn their heads to the sun, soaking up the glory of each ray, and we enjoy being in the spotlight of its warmth.

But the blistering orb has a sobering effect upon our pups, for while they enjoy the radiance of the outside world, their coats become heavy, their internal temperature soars and unlike us, they can only stay cool by sweating through paws and nose.

The toll of summer can deal a harsh hand to freedom-loving hounds. While exercise is still important, walking in the midday sun should be avoided. Instead, try cooler options. A gentle early morning stroll through the woods provides plenty of shade for your pooch to enjoy. River walks that allow a quick and rejuvenating splash are also top dog. Keep your furry friend hydrated with fresh water, ice licks and frozen treats and let them rest, especially during the hottest parts of the day. Read up on the signs of heatstroke, which include excessive panting, drooling, pacing and reddened gums. If lazing the days away in a snoozy siesta is their bag, let sleeping dogs lie.

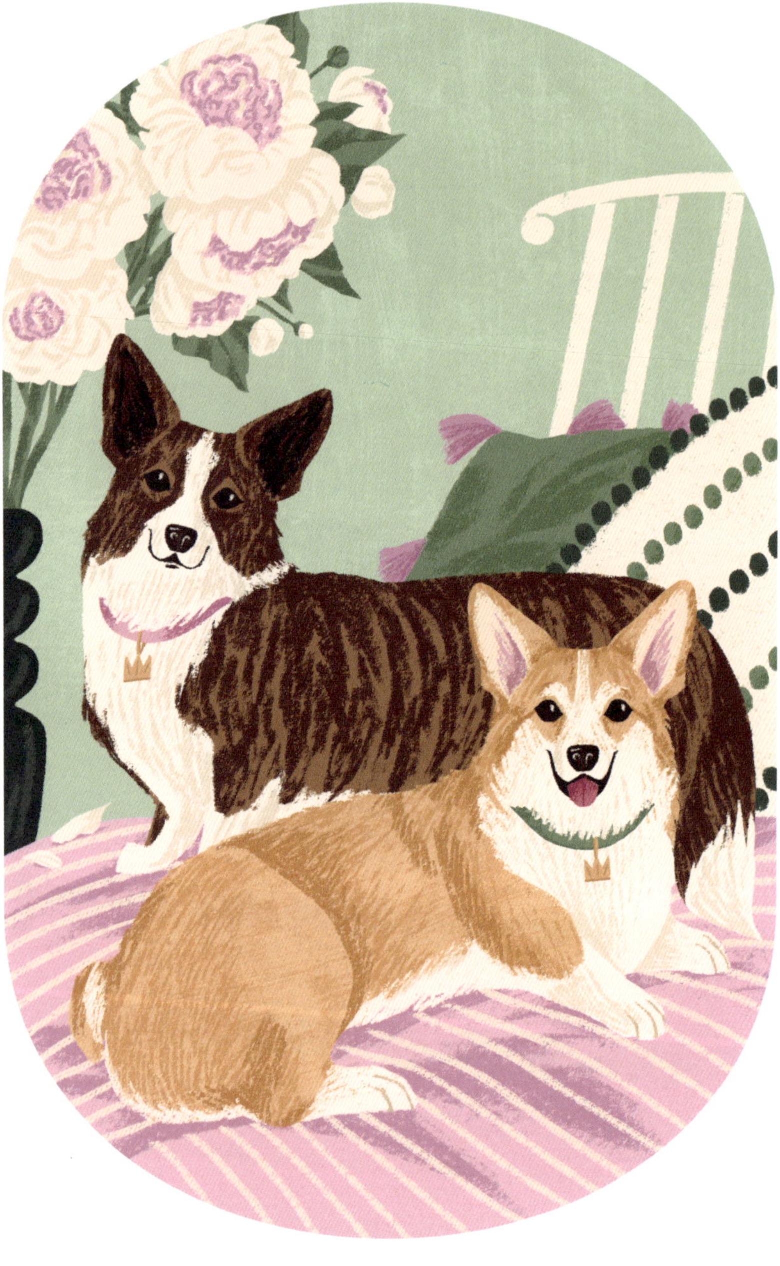

JUNE

JUNE

DOG OF THE MONTH

CORGI

This petite herding dog hails from Wales, and has a curious and magical history. Its name means 'dwarf dog', and refers to its impish yet stocky size. Thought to be excellent working dogs, Corgis were used for centuries to keep sheep in check by nipping at their heels.

There are two distinct breeds: the Pembroke and the Cardigan, named after the areas from which they come. However, the true roots of the Corgi are diverse. There are a number of theories, with some believing that they were brought to British shores by the Vikings, making them descendants of the Swedish cattle dog known as the Vallhund. Others believe it was Flemish weavers who set up home in Wales around the 12th century and brought the diminutive breed with them.

By far the most interesting is the theory that they are companions to the fae. Used as tiny steeds, they would carry their fairy hosts upon their backs, and ride into battle or transport their quarry over long distances. This belief is supported by the saddle-shaped marking that appears on the shoulders of the Pembroke's coat. Whatever the true origins of this breed, one thing is certain: they are quick, nimble and extremely clever, which means they need regular exercise and stimulation to keep them feeling on top form. These pint-sized pups are popular with everyone, including the British monarchy.

DOG SUPERSTITION

GOOD (LUCK) DOGGIES

While many dog superstitions seem to focus on impending doom, our canines can create good fortune simply by being there at the right time. In some countries, like Japan and France, black dogs are an auspicious sign, particularly for those who are down on their luck. If one appears to the person, it's an omen that things are going to turn around for them.

Greyhounds were prized for their character and virtue, and were often used as emblems in tombs to show that the deceased was a person of honour. If a dog should lick a newborn babe, then the child would grow up to be strong, and a quick healer. Any dog that enters the home is thought to herald good fortune, but should it be a Shih Tzu, a person will be extra blessed as these cute pooches are considered extremely lucky and carry positive energy with them, according to popular Chinese belief.

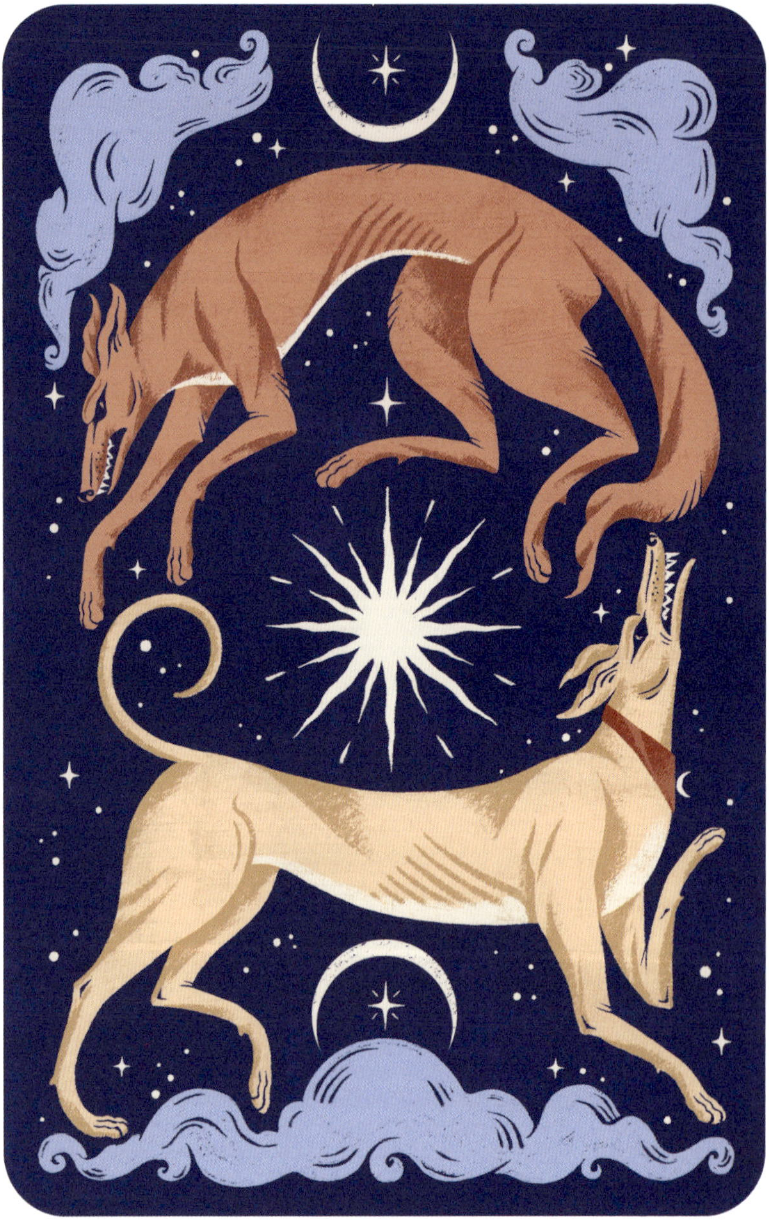

CANINE MYTH
LAELAPS

The legendary hound Laelaps often features in Greek mythology. This boundless beauty was forever destined to catch his prey. Those at his mercy soon discovered there was no escaping his clutches, for there was nothing that this dog couldn't hunt. A magical beast whose name means 'hurricane', Laelaps was gifted by the great Greek god Zeus to the princess Europa. The god, who had transformed into a bull and whisked Europa to the island of Crete, was so enamoured with Europa that he bestowed her with presents at every turn. He wanted her to be safe in his absence, so he left Laelaps as her trusty guardian.

Over the years, Europa prospered and married king Asterion, and their son Mino inherited Laelaps. But the hound was destined to move between owners, often gifted as a reward for services rendered. Soon, Laelaps was commandeered to hunt the Teumessian Fox, a fiendish man-eating creature who had terrorized the city of Thebes for many years. The fox, being no ordinary monster, was destined to never be caught, and Laelaps was destined to always catch his prey, so the two created a never-ending paradox. Zeus, realizing the folly of the situation, stepped in, transforming both creatures into constellations known as Canis Major (Laelaps) and Canis Minor (the Teumessian Fox).

JUNE

CLEVER DOG
TWITCHY PAWS

Dogs spend half their day snoozing, with some breeds exceeding this amount, and they go through similar sleep cycles to us. Dogs have phases of lighter sleep and wakefulness, and they also experience periods of REM (rapid eye movement) sleep. During this time, it's likely that they'll slip into dream, and you'll be able to tell from the twitching and flinching that they do. Just like humans, dogs can have happy dreams where they recall treasured memories, or re-enact escapades from their day like a fun game of ball in the park. They can also experience nightmares based on any fears they've inherited, and will often relive traumatic events in their dreams. It's thought that smaller dogs tend to dream more than larger breeds, and puppies also have more nightly adventures than fully grown canines.

CANINE CHAT
WINKS AND SNEEZES

Sometimes a dog will do something that seems perfectly ordinary to us, but it's actually a form of communication. A simple sneeze could have many causes, and if your pooch is doing this often, then it's best to get them checked out by a vet. But medical issues aside, it also a way of saying to you, 'Hey, I'm here and I want to play!' If your dog is sneezing when faced with another pup, then it could still be a form of communication and their way of saying, 'I'm no threat,' or, 'I'd like to get to know you better.' A wink may mean they've got something in their eye, but it can also be a way of showing submission. Dogs can use this facial inflection to break their gaze, and show they mean no harm.

PUPPY POWER MOVES

SIT!

If you've ever tried dog yoga, you know the benefits of performing moves and stretches with your pooch. You might not be able to get them to do what you want, but this easy pose is something that takes little effort, and will boost loving energy and help you both relax.

- Sit on the floor in a cross-legged position, next to your pup.
- Roll your shoulders back and elongate your spine.
- Place one hand on your dog's chest, and the other over your heart.
- Breathe deeply, and exhale for four long counts.
- Sit comfortably in this position and repeat for as long as you like, and enjoy the comfort this brings.

JUNE

DOG FUN

MAKE YOUR OWN SNUFFLE MAT

Sometimes the simplest games are the best, especially for younger dogs who are just learning about the world. Puppies are naturally curious, and everything is a new adventure. To stimulate their hunting instincts, play an easy game of find the treat by unfolding an old towel before them. Scatter some of their favourite biscuit treats in the centre, then roll it up loosely. Watch as your pup investigates with their nose and slowly unravels layers of towel to get to their prize. This game is great for youngsters as there are no sharp edges for them to hurt themselves. Older dogs too will appreciate the gentle nature of this exercise.

DOG SPELL

SPELL TO HELP EASE SEPARATION ANXIETY

Some dogs find it hard to be alone, and get distressed if their owner leaves them for any length of time. This type of separation anxiety can be combatted with careful training techniques. Use this simple spell alongside more traditional solutions to help your pooch feel more secure.

You will need: a cup of chamomile tea, a neckerchief

- Brew a cup of chamomile tea, and sit at a table with the neckerchief and cup in front of you.

- Hold the neckerchief in both hands over the steam rising from the cup.

JUNE

- As you do this, say, 'Infused and soothed, the spirit calmed, no longer fearful or alarmed. Should I step away or disappear, know in your heart, I'm always here.'
- Take the neckerchief and wrap it around your neck as you continue to sip the brew. Picture your pooch and imagine giving them a loving cuddle to soothe their fears.
- Continue to wear the neckerchief throughout the day, then the next time you need to leave your dog alone for any length of time, remove it and tie it around your dog's neck.
- The calming aroma of chamomile coupled with your own scent should go some way to making your pup feel safe and secure when you're not around.

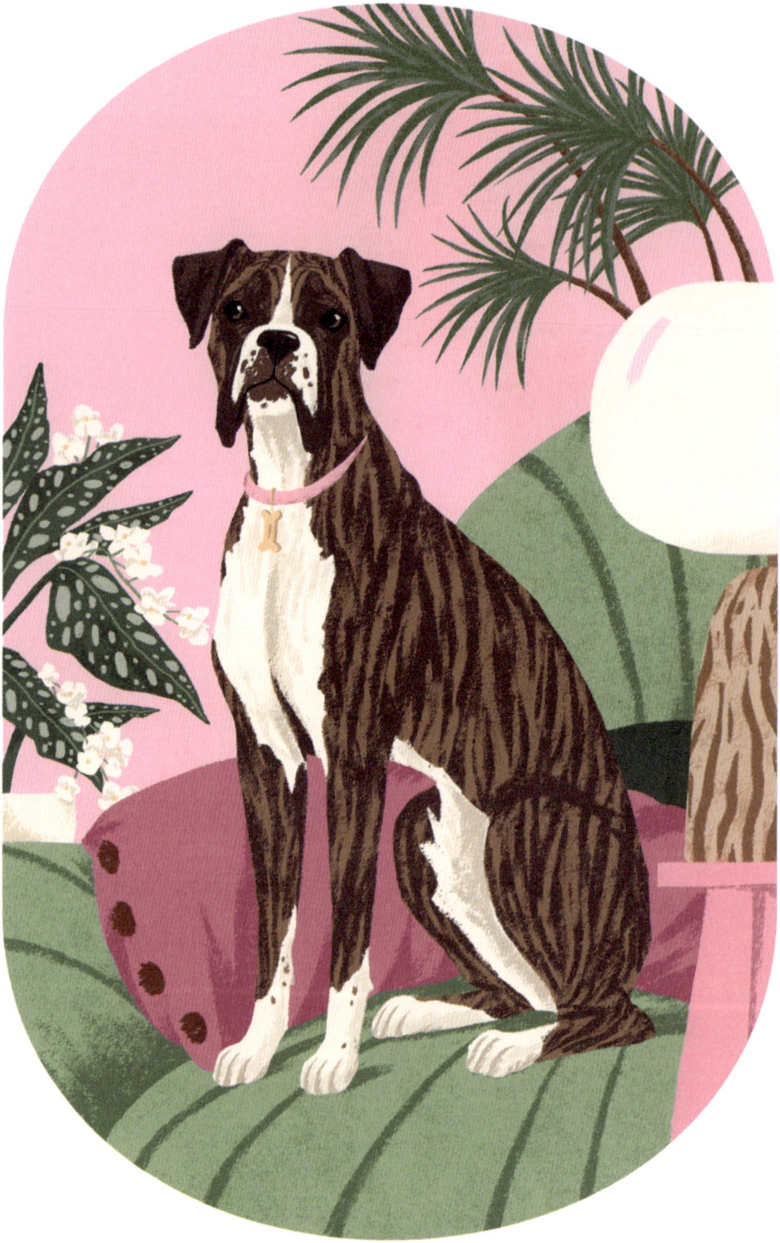

JULY

JULY

DOG OF THE MONTH
BOXER

Rampant and rambunctious, the beautiful Boxer is a boundless well of energy, keeping its youthful spirit long into adulthood. This handsome pooch is a bundle of fun, which is quite at odds with its original purpose as a bull-baiting dog.

Thought to be the descendant of an ancient breed of battle dogs used in the Assyrian Empire, descendents of today's Boxer were no strangers to war and were frequent fighters, accompanying their masters on the battlefield. Over the years, this Assyrian breed evolved and became known in 19th century Europe as the Bullenbeisser, meaning 'bull biter'. This noble pooch was often used in big game hunting, and images of a Boxer-like dog feature on old tapestries that depict boar hunts of the era. When such pastimes fell out of favour, the Bullenbeisser became a family dog, and over time, was mixed with other European breeds to create the modern-day Boxer. With a long career as a working dog, the loyal Boxer loves to serve, and played a key role during World War I and II, delivering packages and fighting on the front line.

Being full of vitality, this pup loves the company of children; they match the Boxer's vivacious energy, and also bring out the Boxer's protective nature. As a breed, it needs little maintenance. Their shiny short-haired coat takes care of itself, but while grooming isn't an issue, this pooch can have dental issues, so regular teeth brushing is a must.

DOG SUPERSTITION
HAIR OF THE DOG

Throughout the world, it was commonly thought that most stray dogs had rabies. This medieval belief tainted many cultures and caused some strange superstitions. Canines were often slaughtered even if they seemed healthy because it was thought that the smallest bite could turn sour if the dog should develop the disease in later years. Those who had been bitten by a rabid dog would look to the animal for a magical cure, and would be force-fed its hairs, or a piece of its liver to banish the disease. Equally, dogs were seen as charms to cure all ills and used in spells to heal any kind of malady. Hairs would be plucked from the sick person and then fed to the dog between slices of bread. It was thought that this ritual transferred the illness to the pooch so that the person could recover swiftly.

CLEVER DOG
SPOTS AND SENSES

Puppies, though beautiful, are not fully developed at birth. They start their life missing some key senses, being both completely deaf and also unable to see properly. Their eyes open properly around the 12-week mark. Other changes occur too, with some breeds like the Shih Tzu changing the colour of their coat by their first birthday. Dalmatian puppies are the real shapeshifters of the dog world; they begin life totally white and only develop their customary spotted coat as they get older.

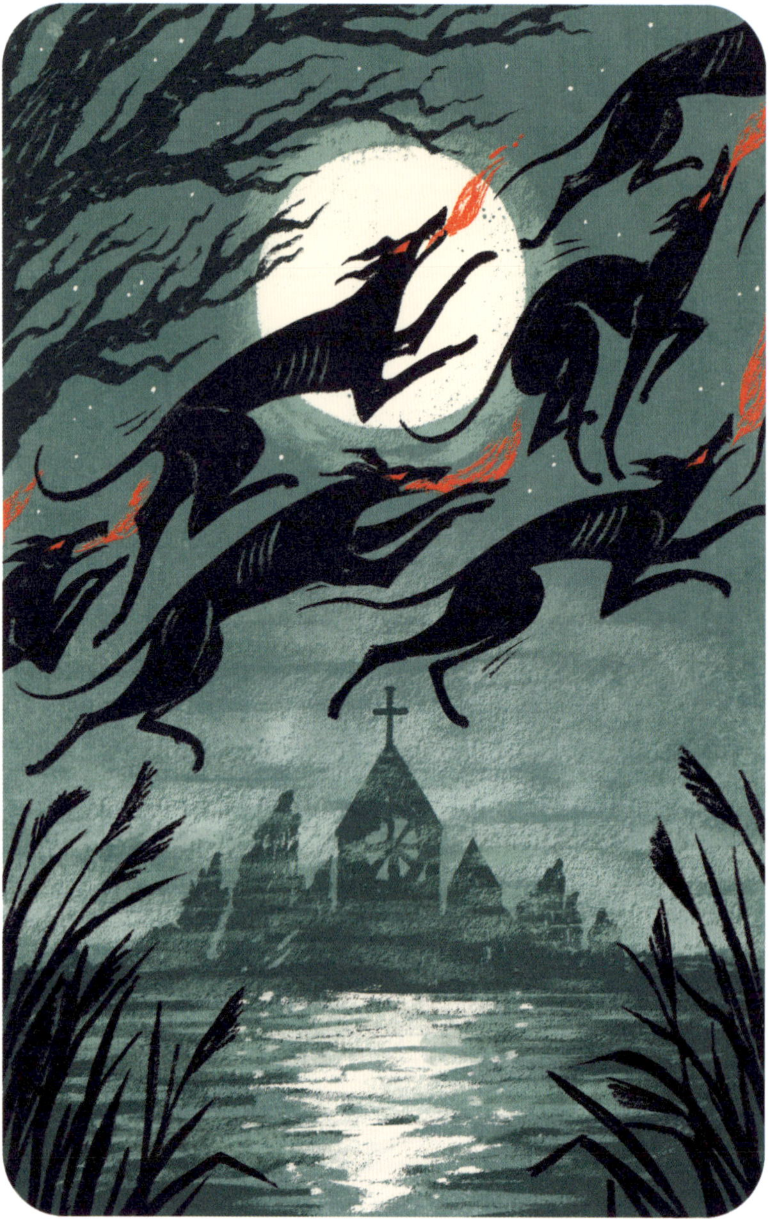

CANINE MYTH

DANDO'S DOGS

Should you wander the windswept Cornish moors upon a stormy night, you might witness Dando's dogs galloping through the air. This terrifying sight is not for the faint-hearted, for these canines are spectral beings who breathe fire as they run. That said, they are only being faithful to their owner, a sinful priest who should have known better than to dabble with the Devil.

As the story goes, Dando the priest, despite his allegiance to the church, enjoyed the hunt, and would venture out on a Sunday, the day of rest. After yet another successful expedition, he returned and demanded alcohol to quell his passion. Many drinks were served, but Dando was not satiated and called for more. His companions shook their heads. They had nothing more to give for he had drank them dry. Dando, unfazed by this, smiled a wicked smile and said, 'If there are no more drinks on earth then I shall go to Hell.'

At that point, a stranger entered the inn and offered him a swig from his flask, to which the priest greedily accepted. It's thought that the stranger, likely the Devil, then whisked Dando to Hell, for he was never seen again. His dogs gave chase, but it was futile. Even so, they continue to run, scouring the deserted landscape at the dawn of every Sunday in search of their wayward master.

JULY

CANINE CHAT
SLEEPY HEADS

A dog's sleeping position reveals much about its state of mind and how it feels in the moment. Like humans, pups move about in their sleep, and often have poses that they favour the most. Dogs who like to sleep in the sphinx position, crouched on all fours with their head resting on their front paws, are still semi-alert. They're relaxed but not ready to submit to the snooze in case they're needed. While this is a popular position for working and guard dogs, high energy pooches tend to prefer the Superman pose, flat out on their belly with paws and legs stretched out. They can dip into a deep doze, but also be ready to play at the drop of a hat. A side-sleeping dog is feeling super-chilled, and is most likely to dream in this position, while the canine that curls into a ball may be feeling a little vulnerable or cold, and is protecting their most vulnerable bits while preserving heat.

PUPPY POWER MOVES

THE TAIL CHASE

Dogs are obsessed with tails, especially their own. From chasing it in endless circles to checking it out, a pooch's derrière is a thing of fascination. Take inspiration from these twisting movements to hone and tone your waist and improve flexibility.

- Stand with your feet hip width apart.
- Place your hands on your hips.
- Take a long slow breath in, and as you exhale begin to twist from side to side at the waist, rotating your hips as you go. Make it your aim to look directly behind you, and extend each spin so that you can feel the pull on your hips.
- Continue to breathe deeply as you twist, and gradually pick up speed.
- Repeat this motion for a minute or two. Then, when you're ready, slowly reduce speed until you come to a halt.
- Breathe, relax and give your limbs a shake.

JULY

DOG FUN
WALKIES

There's one word that's sure to spark excitement in most pups, and that's 'walkies'. Dogs love to get out and about. It counteracts boredom and allows them to engage with their surroundings. Naturally inquisitive, they enjoy using their senses, and the outside world is full of new scents and sounds to explore. A brisk walk also provides the opportunity for some human and dog bonding time, and helps to strengthen the emotional connection between you, which can help with behavioural problems. Keep walks fun and stimulating by mixing things up. Take a different route and vary the terrain, so if you usually take your pooch to the park, find a wood or natural reserve and have a ramble together. You'll both benefit from the new challenge this provides.

DOG SPELL

SPELL TO HELP YOU FIND THE RIGHT DOG

If you're thinking of getting a pooch but you're not sure what type to go for, then this spell could help. It will focus your mind and open your heart so that you'll know when the right pup for you has come along.

You will need: a book of different dog breeds, a lighter or matches, a pink candle, a piece of rose quartz

It's best to perform this spell on a Friday so that you can tap into the loving energy of the planet Venus.

- To begin, set the book in front of you and light the pink candle. Pink is the colour associated with the heart chakra, and this will help you tune in to loving energy.
- Close your eyes and hold the quartz crystal over the centre of your chest. Let the magical energy of the crystal fill you up with every breath that you take.
- Set your intention to find the right dog for you by saying, 'The right pup for me, I'll know when I see. Heart to heart, together we will be.'
- Open your eyes and place the crystal on top of the book for a couple of minutes.
- When you're ready, pick up the book and let it fall open. See what kind of dog features on the pages and this may give you an idea of the perfect breed for you.
- To finish, let the candle burn down.
- Repeat the words from this spell before you visit any rescue centres or breeders.

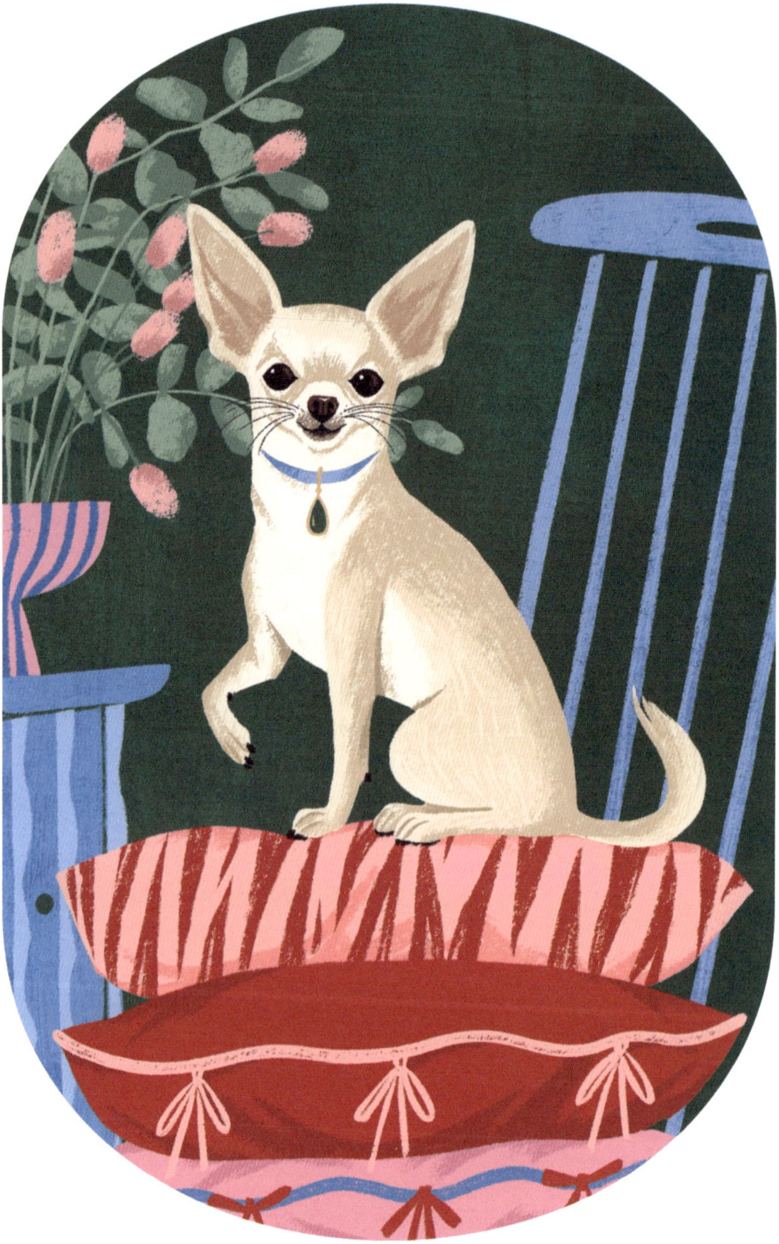

AUGUST

AUGUST

DOG OF THE MONTH
CHIHUAHUA

This friendly, chatty breed is a mystical powerhouse according to folklore. Being at least 3,000 years old, the Chihuahua is one of the oldest dog breeds and hales from Mexico. A descendent of the Techichi, a tiny stocky dog with huge ears that was bred by the Toltec people, these little pups were believed to possess supernatural powers, including the ability to predict the future. As such, they were considered sacred and prized for their magical gifts. Should the pooch be blessed with a reddish coat then it could also navigate the Underworld.

Popular with Aztec nobles, the Chihuahua, which evolved after crossbreeding with hairless dogs, was often sacrificed when its owner died and was buried or cremated with them. Thanks to its knowledge of the afterlife, the pup, in spirit form, would help its human swim across the river to the Underworld, carrying the person's spiritual essence upon its back. These beguiling dogs were often used like currency, and those in a position of power would trade them in order to build their own pack.

Today the Chihuahua is adored for its diminutive features and charming personality. Whether long- or short-haired, it's easy to groom, adaptable when it comes to a living environment and full of playful energy. What this pup lacks in size it makes up for in its larger-than-life character!

DOG SUPERSTITION

WEATHER REPORTERS

Dogs have long been associated with weather forecasting. Since the Middle Ages, folks from around the world have looked to their pooch for divine inspiration when it comes to meteorological changes. It was commonly thought that if a dog was happily munching the grass or laying on its back with its paws in the air, then torrential rain was on the way. But should a pup sit with its front paws crossed, then it was likely that the showers would be light and only passing through. If a dog refused to go out or sat under the kitchen table, then cold weather was around the corner.

Although there's no scientific evidence for these superstitions, it's true that dogs can sniff out changes in atmosphere and often sense when something is afoot. Their incredible hearing also allows them to hear things in the distance, so a dog will often pace and tremble to indicate a storm coming.

AUGUST

CANINE MYTH

EL LUISON

The Guarani people of South America have a long history of mystical beasts and legends, but one of the most terrifying is of the black hound known as El Luison. It was a monstrous creature thought to be the offspring of the evil spirit Tau and Kerana, the granddaughter of the first humans to walk the earth. This beast was born from a violent act, for Tau forced himself upon Kerana, although in some tales it was said that she secretly agreed to the union and that they were married. Between them, they had seven children, each one equally revolting thanks to a curse that the goddess Arasy placed upon them. The children became the seven monsters of Guarani mythology.

El Luison was the final child, and the most fiendish in form and behaviour. Known as the Lord of Death, El Luison's appearance was an evil omen, and thought to symbolize the passing of someone closeby. Once the person had died, the beast dog would feed upon their corpse and soul. As the myth evolved the creature also changed, and became a werewolf stalking its victims. It was able to adopt human form until the night of the full moon when it transformed into a demonic dog-like entity. Should you happen to see El Luison the worst thing you can do is panic, for the fear will eventually drive you insane.

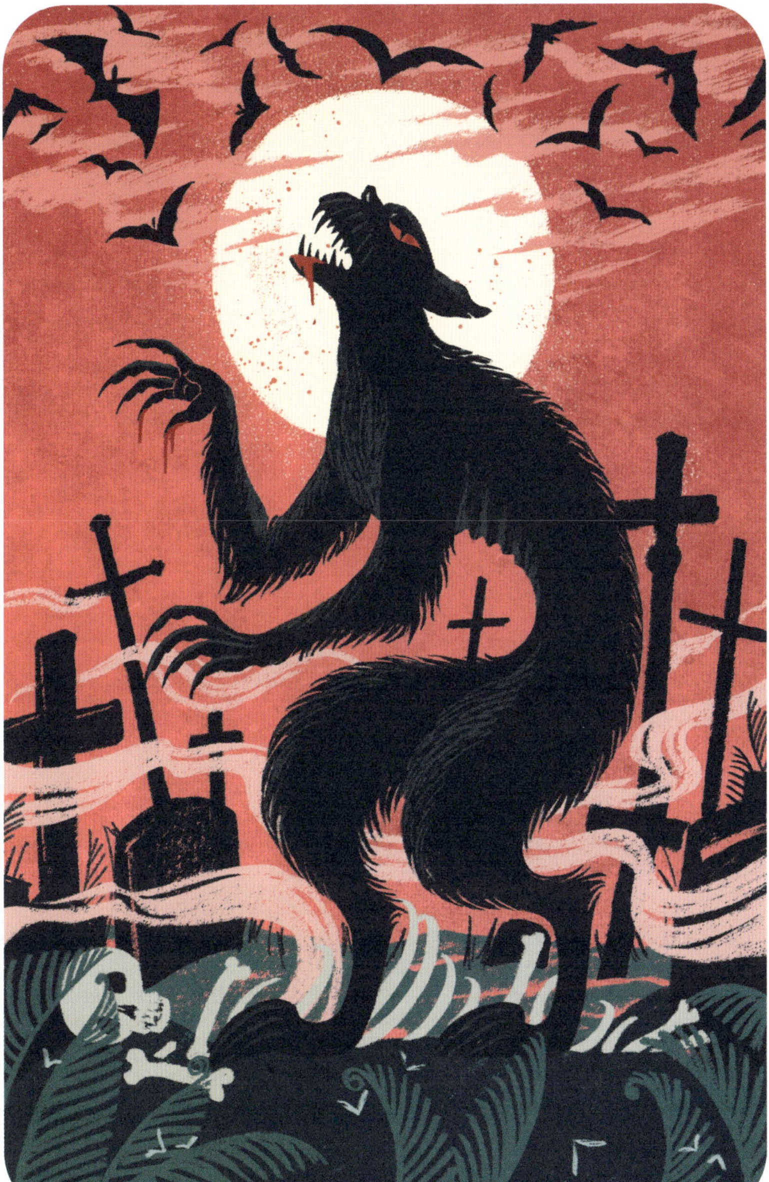

AUGUST

CLEVER DOG

LOVED-UP POOCHES

When a dog stares lovingly at its owner, it really is feeling all the feels. According to research, during these moments the levels of oxytocin in a dog's system increase to suggest the pooch is loved up. While that may cause you to want to give your dog a cuddle, resist the urge. Dogs are not fans of hugging. The action of placing a limb around your pooch can be seen as dominant and even aggressive, and can make them feel uncomfortable. Look for signs of stress such as constant lip-licking or the folding of ears, as these can reveal what your pup is really thinking. Instead, opt for a belly rub, which is more agreeable to the average canine.

CANINE CHAT

THE ZOOMIES

Dogs do the strangest things, but there is usually meaning behind the madness. As an owner, it's good to keep an eye on their behaviour, as it could indicate deeper health issues. That said, there are some things dogs do that can be easily explained by mood and humour. Should a dog start racing around at top speed, otherwise known as the zoomies, then it's down to high spirits. They're feeling good and full of energy and they want the world to know. Think of this as the canine version of a dancefloor shimmy.

A dog that chases its tail is also feeling happy and playful, but should the tail chasing become obsessive, there could be something else going on, like an inner ear problem. When a dog circles before settling down, it's an instinctual behaviour, likely inherited from wolves who would do this to prepare a safe spot to rest.

PUPPY POWER MOVES

THE BIG STRETCH

Dog's love to lounge on their side. It's the perfect position for comfort and provides a good stretch. Take inspiration from their sideways moves, with this simple exercise that works your flanks, legs and lower back.

- Lay on your side with your knees bent and pulled in to your tummy.
- Relax your arms and bring your palms together near your face.
- Take a deep breath in and as you release it, stretch your arms and legs out in front of you.
- Inhale again and raise your top leg slightly in the air. Hold, then release as you exhale.
- Draw your legs and arms back towards your body and relax.
- Repeat on the other side.

AUGUST

DOG FUN

DOGGY DANCING

Dogs love to dance especially if it's with their human family. It's a fun way to exercise and bond, and the good news is that it doesn't matter what you look like. Your pooch will love it. Clear some space and make sure anything that might get in the way is tucked away. Stick on your favourite track, pick something upbeat, and encourage your dog to join in with the groove. You can do this by spinning their favourite toy in the air or waving a treat above their head. Most pups will join in with the action because it looks like you're playing a game. Make the most of this time and teach them some new tricks, like encouraging them to spring in the air or roll over.

DOG SPELL

SPELL TO COMMUNICATE WITH YOUR PUP

Dogs have a sixth sense. They're able to pick up on how you are feeling and communicate their love and understanding in non-verbal ways, and this can be reciprocated. This spell helps to trigger your intuition and open up the channels of psychic communication between you both.

You will need: lavender essential oil, a small dish of warm water, a spoon

This spell is best performed on any evening when the moon is waxing or full, as this will help the flow of psychic energy.

- Sit next to, or close to your dog. Try and choose a moment when you're both feeling relaxed.
- Add three drops of the essential oil to the warm water and stir well with the spoon.
- Dip your index finger into the water, then trace a circular shape in the centre of your forehead.
- Keep going over the circle, massaging the area and as you do this, imagine a tiny purple flower bud in this spot. See each petal gradually open until the flower is in full bloom.
- Now repeat the process with your dog. Dip your finger in the water, then gently trace a circle on their head. Do this lightly and turn it into a fun head massage.
- When you've finished, simply sit and relax in their company. Breathe deeply and notice any thoughts or feelings that arise; these could be psychic messages from your pup.

AUTUMN

Glorius autumn sweeps through the landscape casting a golden haze wherever it goes. Its burnished skirts swish, and with each flurry it brings change and a general slowing down. The earth is turning its attention inwards, retreating to conserve energy and warmth, and all the creatures upon it feel the difference. The timbre of the trees turns too, and the once-fresh, verdant leaves begin to dry and form a patchwork canopy of burnt amber, rose red and burnished bronze. The seasonal gifts are many – from conkers and pine cones to jewel-like berries that line the bushes – and while it's a joy to see, the wonderland of the woods becomes a dangerous place for our furry friends.

That's not to say that your dog won't enjoy a ramble with you close at hand, but it's wise to keep an eye on their foraging. Fallen fruits with their stones and pips contain toxins, which could make your pup ill. Acorns too are full of tannic acid, which will give your dog an upset tummy. Mushrooms love a damp environment, and while some are edible, it can be hard to identify the deadlier variety, so it's best to keep your pooch on a lead and instead enjoy a brisk stroll and some playful leaf-kicking fun together.

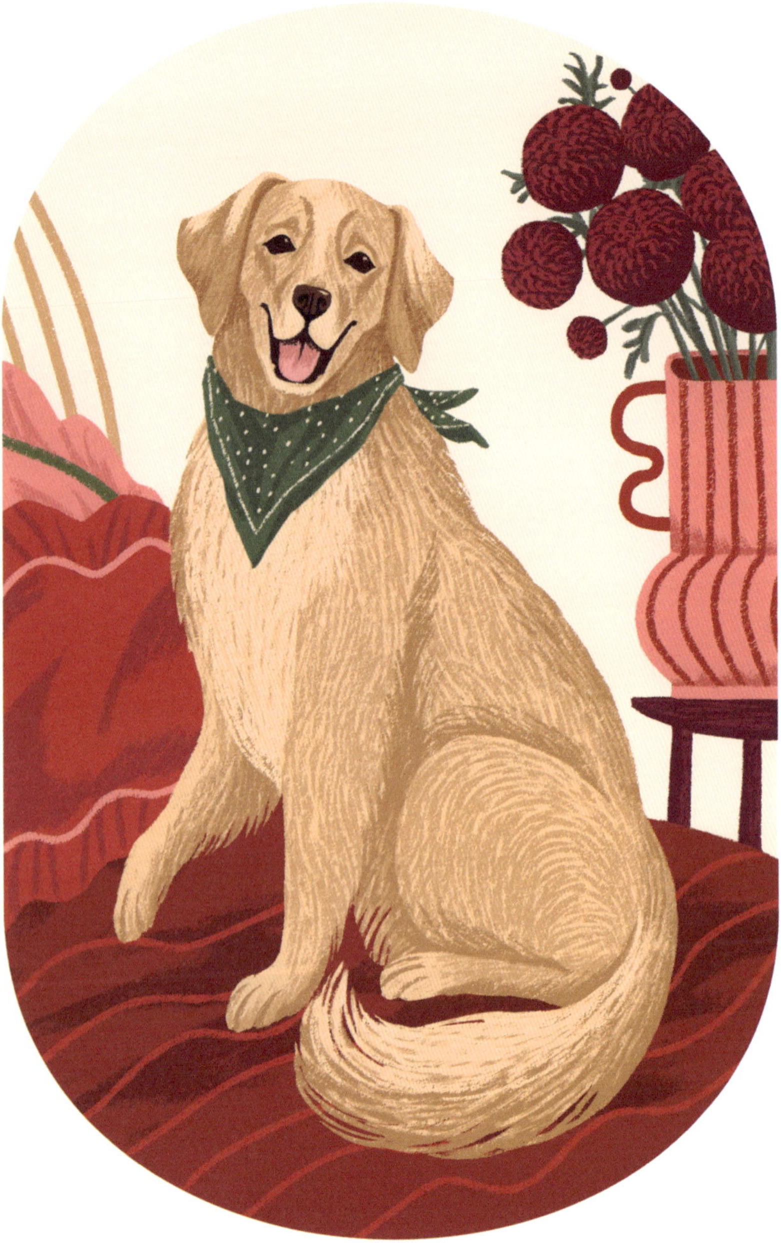

SEPTEMBER

SEPTEMBER

DOG OF THE MONTH

GOLDEN RETRIEVER

It's thanks to Dudley Majoribanks, a Scottish nobleman otherwise known as Lord Tweedmouth, that this beautiful loving companion exists. Determined to create the perfect hunting partner, he set about making a supreme retriever by breeding a Flat-coated Retriever named Nous with a Tweed Water Spaniel called Belle. The event, which happened in 1868, would change history and spawn the gentle, outgoing breed we know and love today.

Nous, a tiny yellow puppy in a litter of black, had a distinctive hue that made him stand out from the crowd. But his origins are the real mystery. Some believe that Nous belonged to a Russian circus trainer who had planned to include him in his act. According to folklore, Lord Tweedmouth stumbled across the young dog in Brighton, England and swiftly purchased him. Other theories suggest that Nous belonged to a group of travelling gypsies who crossed paths with the lord on his travels. Whatever the truth, at the time, lighter-skinned retrievers were often disposed of, as there was a belief that they couldn't hunt as well as their black counterparts. Nous was lucky to be alive, and even more so to have found a home of such standing.

Today, retrievers are prized for their lustrous golden coat, muscular build and unfailing loyalty. These charmers are intelligent, inquisitive and devoted to their owners.

DOG SUPERSTITION

LUCKY MUCK

Dog owners can't help feeling lucky. Pups are so loving and loyal that being in their company lifts the spirits, which in turn promotes positive energy. It's no wonder it's considered lucky to have a dog in the home.

That said, there's a rather strange and somewhat smelly superstition that brings an abundance of good fortune. In France it's believed that if you step in dog poop you will be blessed with luck, and may even experience a windfall of some kind. If you're inclined to put this to the test there is a rule to follow: the luck only works if it's your left foot. Putting your right foot forward and into the muck has little effect, and will just leave you with a messy shoe.

CLEVER DOG

BIG BRAINS

If you've noticed that your dog seems to know exactly when you're due home, or if you're late for mealtimes, it's thanks to an impressive range of superpowers. Scientists believe that dogs think about a range of different things throughout the day, including their environment, social relationships and wellbeing. They're also blessed with an excellent long-term memory, and have the ability to recall up to 250 different places and people. Couple this with their circadian rhythm, an inherent internal mechanism that helps them tell time during the day, and you'll realize that the average canine is a bit of a brainbox.

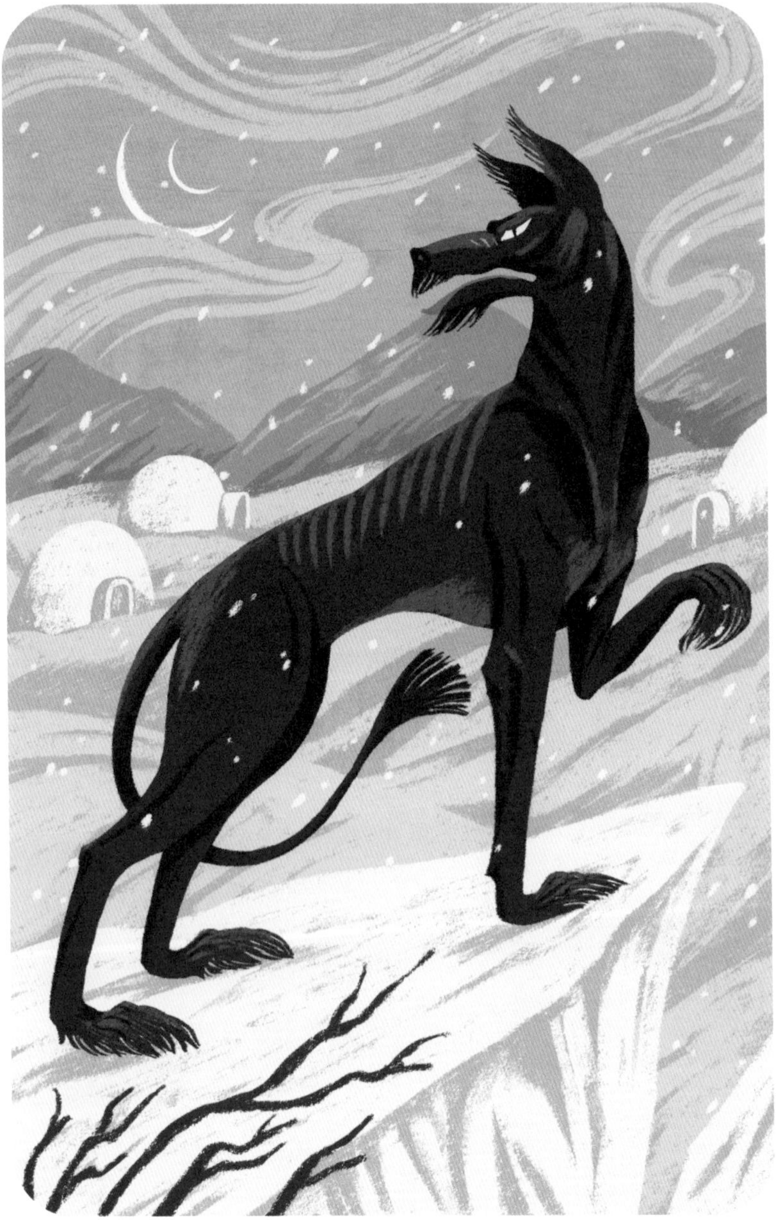

CANINE MYTH

THE QIQIRN

This ghostly entity haunts Inuit folklore, and has become something of a legend among the Eskimos. It appears when you least expect it – a dark, monstrous dog of gigantic proportions. While it's certainly canine, it's almost hairless; only the tips of its enormous ears, and its tail, feet and mouth have fur. The Qiqirn may be naked, but it doesn't feel the cold. It uses its hairy paws to brush away the snow so that it can move stealthily through the icy landscape. Although it prefers isolation, this creature has been known to cross the path of humans and other dogs. When it does it has a strange effect, causing its victims to fit, and go insane. Some suggest that these bizarre fits are actually some form of shamanic journey, which results in the person losing their mind. Either way, the Qiqirn is actually scared of humans and tries to avoid them at all costs.

Writers and storytellers have often featured this mystical beast in tales, where it appears in a more positive light, leading travellers who are lost in a snowstorm back to safety. In this guise, the creature, still hairless and toothless, has extra limbs and two heads.

SEPTEMBER

CANINE CHAT

POORLY PUPS

It's important to know the signs that your pup is under the weather. Sometimes, these can be obvious, like shifts in appetite and strange toilet habits, but dogs have a tendency to hide vulnerability, a behaviour they inherited from their wild ancestors. All dogs like a snooze, but if your pooch is super-sleepy and has less energy than usual, it could be a sign of an underlying problem.

Similarly, if your pup seems more fired up, or begins to twitch, they could be experiencing a seizure. Snapping at the air or obsessive tail chasing could be a problem, and excessive paw or forearm licking might be an allergy. A tilted head is cute, but if your pup remains in this position, they could have an ear infection. Be aware of what is normal for your dog and if you do notice anything unusual, get them checked by a vet.

PUPPY POWER MOVES
THE CHILLED CANINE

Want to feel grounded and strong? Get close to the earth and relax in this dog-inspired pose. It takes just a couple of minutes to perform, and coupled with some deep breathing will help you centre yourself and relieve stress.

You will need: a yoga mat

- Get on your hands and knees on the mat.
- Keep your back straight and tuck your tummy in. If it helps, picture a pup standing in this position.
- Take a long breath in, tighten your core, then release your breath, letting your tummy fall towards the floor.
- Lift your chin and gaze upwards and hold this position.
- Inhale again lowering your head and tucking your tummy in, and repeat the process.
- Feel the gentle stretch, and focus on the feel of the floor beneath your hands and legs.

SEPTEMBER

DOG FUN

CREATE A SNIFFARI

Dogs like to sniff. It's how they make sense of the world, and it also helps them to relax by lowering their heart rate. Sniffing also releases dopamine into their system, a brain chemical that generates happy feelings for your pup. No wonder they're always doing it. Tap into this pleasure centre of the brain and give your dog a treat by planning a sensory, scented walk.

A fragrant flower garden or park with lots of sweet-scented bedding plants makes the perfect location for this, but if you're feeling green-fingered, why not create your own floral herb patch at home? Lavender, rosemary and mint are easy to plant and give off lots of scent. Flowers like roses, freesias and petunias also have a strong fragrance, and they're all animal-friendly.

DOG SPELL

SPELL TO HELP YOUR DOG GET ON WITH OTHER PEOPLE

Your pooch loves you, but that doesn't mean they're not wary of other people. This can make it awkward at family get-togethers or if you get an unexpected visitor. Behavioural training will help, but to enhance any work that you do, try this simple spell.

You will need: a lighter or matches, a yellow candle, your dog's bowl, their usual food, a spoonful of ground linseed (flaxseed)

This spell is best performed on a Sunday, when the sun's warm influence will help promote feelings of security.

- Light the candle. Yellow is associated with joy and will promote positive energy.
- Make a wish that your dog feels happy, loved and secure at all times.
- Place your dog's empty bowl in front of the candle. Take a minute to visualize all that loving energy filling their bowl. See it as golden light.
- Empty their usual food into the bowl, then sprinkle the ground linseed on top. This nutritious seed is associated with feelings of security and will help your pup feel protected at all times. It's also great for their health, boosting immunity and giving their coat a glow.
- Repeat this spell once a week for a month to see results.

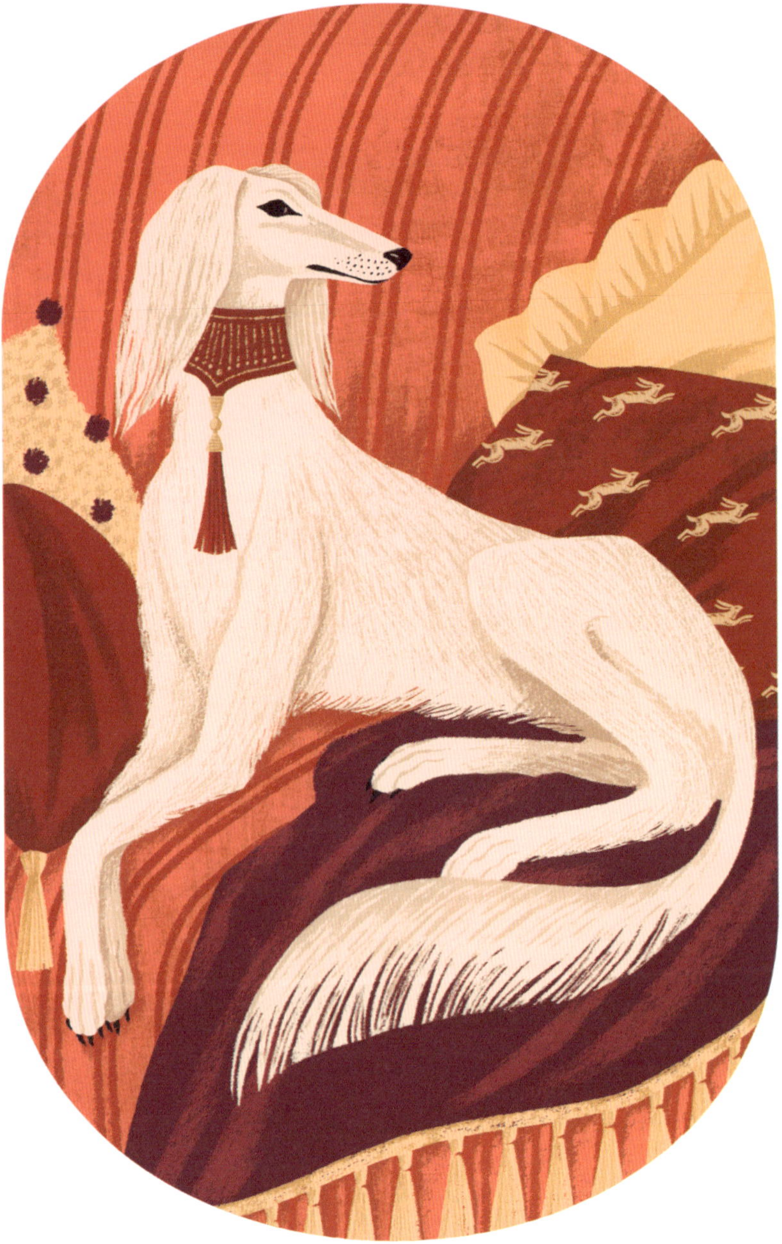

OCTOBER

OCTOBER

DOG OF THE MONTH

SALUKI

This elegant breed of hunting dog dates back at least 5,000 years. Images of slender, feathery-eared Salukis were discovered on mosaics and tomb paintings in the Middle East, and prove the breed's worth among the people of that time. Arab tribesman called the breed 'el hor', meaning 'the noble', and it was valued for its skill and speed. These graceful sight hounds had the ability to spot their prey at a great distance and take chase, bringing down a gazelle in a matter of minutes. It's no surprise that Salukis are still used for hunting today. While they may look bone-thin and fragile, they can reach up to 50 miles per hour, covering tricky and often treacherous terrain.

The ancient Egyptians revered the Saluki, giving them the esteemed title of Royal Dog of Egypt. A beloved companion till death, these dogs were considered part of the family, and were often buried and mummified with their owners.

Because of their heritage and need for speed, Salukis need more exercise than most and value lots of space and freedom to run. That said, they will catch small animals off-lead, so training is vital to instill obedience. With soft, silky coats and large expressive eyes, these beauties can be aloof, but they are also known for their devotion to their owners, making them a loving addition to any family.

DOG SUPERSTITION

HOWLING HOUNDS

A dog's howl is chilling, and seen as a portend of death around the world. Like most things in folklore, there are different theories as to the origins of the howl and what it means. The Norse people associated it with the goddess of war and love Freya, whose job was to collect the souls of brave warriors and take them to Valhalla. She would cruise through the air upon her mighty chariot, which was pulled by two giant blue cats. When earthly dogs saw this feline vision, they reacted by howling loudly.

In England and Ireland, it was believed that the howls were inspired by the Wild Hunt, a pack of ghostly hounds racing through the heavens collecting the souls of the dead.
In America, there are some folk-inspired superstitions that claim the number of howls indicate who may be passing. If it's two then it's a man, and if it's three it's a woman. If the dog howls and looks in your direction then your days are numbered, but should it howl with its back to you, you will be blessed with good fortune.

OCTOBER

CANINE MYTH

CERBERUS

This hound of Hell was the lap dog of the Greek god of death, Hades. A hideous monster, Cerberus was the spawn of the fearsome titan Typhon and his treacherous, snake-like cohort Echidna. Like his parents, Cerberus was terrifying in form, with three hungry heads attached to his giant body. He was also gifted with a mane of hissing snakes, the savage claws of a lion and a serpentine tail. Coupled with his mighty canine build and sharp teeth, it's easy to see why people feared him.

Being such a petrifying sight, it was only fitting that he became the guardian of the Underworld, sitting at the gates to this realm and keeping watch for any errant waifs or strays. He would also patrol the banks of the River Acheron, the waters that the dead souls crossed to reach the gates of the Underworld, looking for any recently deceased stragglers. Constantly baying and howling, the noise he produced made the earth shudder, scaring farmers away from the nearby land. His slobber, of which there was plenty, was thought to contain deadly venom. Stories claim that this became a core ingredient in the spells of the infamous sorceress Medea.

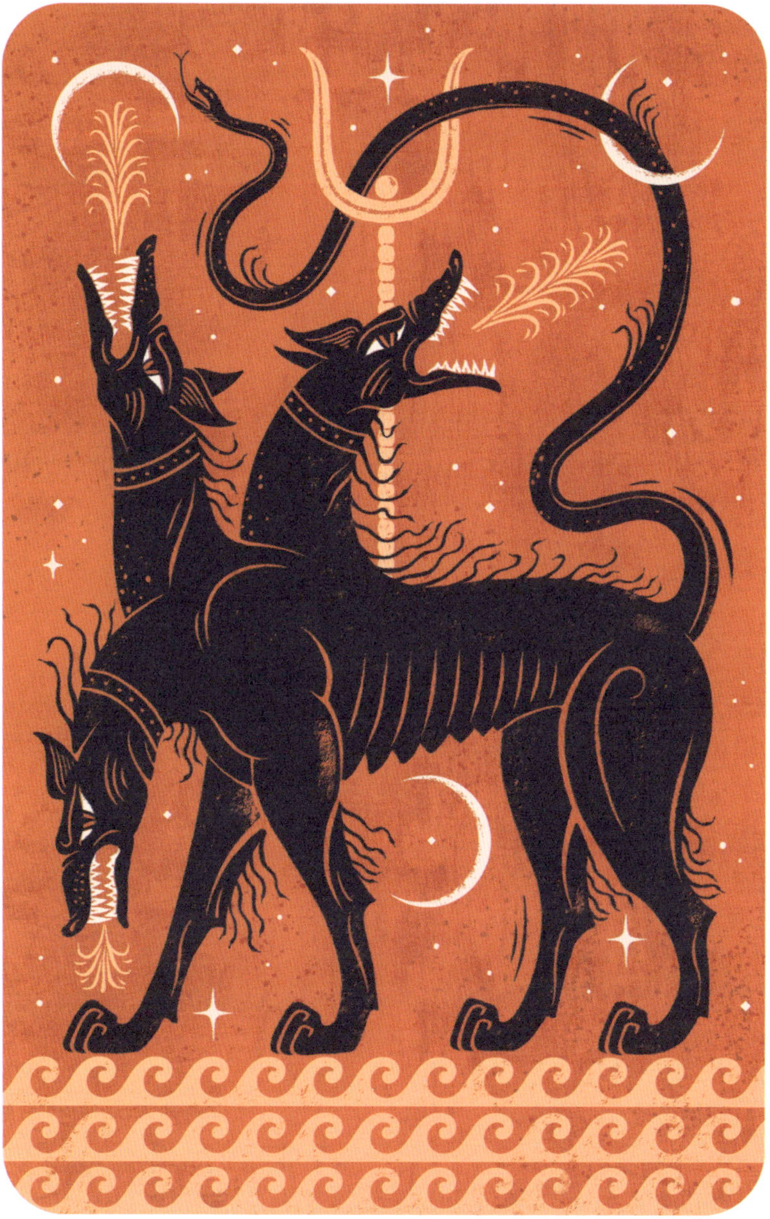

OCTOBER

DOG FUN
BEDTIME SNUGGLES

One of the best things you can do to bring comfort to your pooch is to give them a piece of your clothing. Dogs are driven by scent and love sniffing you, as this tells them where you have been, who you were with and how you are feeling right now. They recognize your scent and it helps to make them feel safe and secure, so it's a great way to treat separation anxiety. Try sleeping in a t-shirt for a couple of nights and then put it in your dog's bed. They'll have hours of fun sniffing it, and it will also make them feel loved.

CANINE CHAT
POSSESSIVE PUPS

Dogs feel a range of emotions, and for the most part they're easy to read. You know that your dog loves you when they want to be near you, whether that's cuddled up close, licking your face or just by your side 24/7. The other side of affection is jealousy, and according to research, the average canine is cursed with the green-eyed monster. It's thought that this is a natural instinct, and because your pup sees you as part of their territory. Signs of a jealous pooch include aggressive behaviour towards other pets and humans, whining when you show affection to others and even toileting issues. Combat this with regular obedience training, and if you have other dogs, include them in training sessions so that your attention is divided between all family members.

PUPPY POWER MOVES
DOWNWARD DOG

The downward dog is a popular canine-inspired yoga move that can help with circulation, strength, flexibility and mental health. While it may be tricky for the complete beginner, it's something you can practice and improve over time.

You will need: a yoga mat

- Begin on all fours with your knees bent and your hands flat on the floor. Keep your wrists in line with your shoulders.
- Take a long breath in, and as you exhale, press into your arms, push your hips upwards into the air and straighten your legs, so you are in a 'V' shape. You should feel the pull along your arms and legs.
- Push back into your heels and begin to slowly walk your feet backwards.
- Hold this position and continue to breathe deeply for 30 seconds to a minute.

OCTOBER

THE DOG'S DINNER

(UN) SOPHISTICATED PALATES

You might think that dogs, having 300 million olfactory receptors in their nose, would have a classy sense of smell, but the opposite is true. Rather than seeking out sublime scents, our pups love anything stinky. From fresh poop to sweaty socks, If something smells gross, then they'll be drawn to it. Scientists believe that when a scent is strong, it lights up the olfactory lobe and works the motor cortex, piquing the curiosity of our pups. This also goes some way to explain why they like to roll in the most disgusting things. Other research suggests this odd behaviour is leftover from their wild ancestors, who, when hunting prey, would roll in carrion or dung to mask their scent.

DOG SPELL

SPELL TO BOOST YOUR DOG'S HEALTH AND VITALITY

Sometimes your pup might need a bit of a boost. Whether they're under the weather or you just want to make sure they're in tip-top condition, this lovely spell will help.

You will need: a piece of tourmaline, a charm bag, a piece of paper and a pen

This spell can be performed any day, but if possible, do it in the evening when there's a crescent moon in the sky, as this is associated with increased energy.

- Place the tourmaline stone inside the charm bag. Tourmaline is associated with protection and vitality. It has the ability to boost the immune system and imbue your pup with positive energy.

- Write a wish for good health on the piece of paper, such as 'I wish my lovely dog [insert their name] good health, happiness and lots of fun.'

- Fold the paper up and put it inside the charm bag. Make sure that the bag is sealed tightly and well-hidden to avoid your dog finding and destroying it.

- Place the bag beneath your dog's bed so that the healing energy of the crystal can do its work when they are asleep.

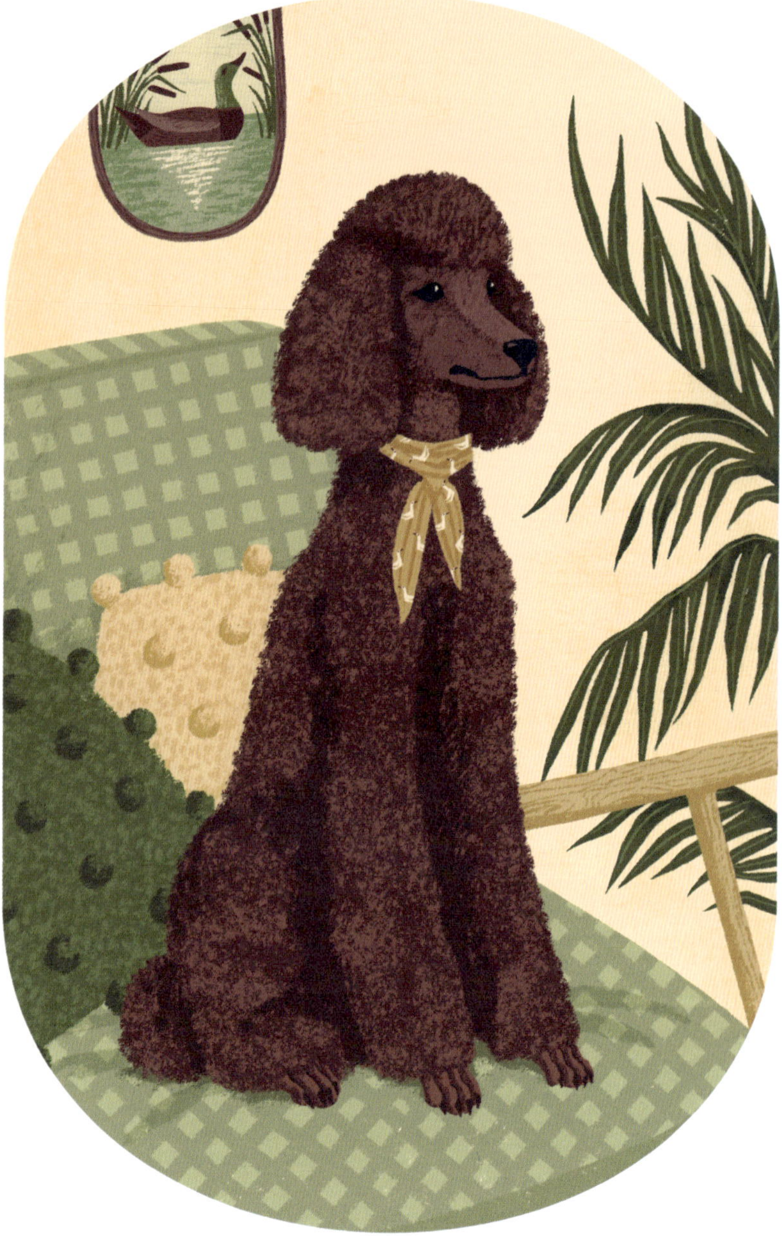

NOVEMBER

NOVEMBER

DOG OF THE MONTH
POODLE

The elegant, fluffy Poodle may seem a lightweight against other more muscular breeds, but don't be fooled. This beautiful pup was originally bred to retrieve waterfowl from icy rivers. A powerful sporting dog, the Poodle finds its origins in Germany where the name *pudel* means 'to play in water'. Its long hairy tresses, which are often primped and coiffured to perfection, were an asset when trying to dry off the dog, as it allowed any water to shed quicker than smoother-haired breeds. The French soon caught on to the Poodle's talents, giving it the moniker Caniche, a combination of the words *canard* meaning 'duck' and *chien* meaning 'dog'. They prized the pup's athletic prowess and appreciated its warm friendly nature, using it to sniff out truffles while also treating it as a family pet.

A favourite of the French aristocracy during the 15th century, the Poodle was clever and had the ability to pick up tricks. It was soon sought after by travelling circuses that roamed Europe at that time. Physically, Poodles can be any size, but the one thing they all have in common is their devotion to their family. Being people-oriented, this spritely breed doesn't do well left alone for long periods of time, and prefers to keep busy, whether that's through playing games, learning new tricks or helping to look after the children. The Poodle is always raring to go.

DOG SUPERSTITION

ON THE LOOSE

Dogs run a lot, so it's not surprising that there are a number of odd superstitions about this. If a couple is on a date and a strange dog runs between their legs, then it's highly unlikely that the relationship will go the distance. Similarly, if the dog happens to run between the legs of a couple in an established relationship, then a quarrel is imminent. If a pup decides to only run between the woman's legs, then she may have to deal with the wrath of her father or romantic partner. That said, if a strange dog should run towards you, it can also be a positive omen, and suggest good times are on the way. Finally, if an errant pooch decides to run on the field during a baseball match, it's particularly bad luck for the batting team, probably because the dog may decide to join in the game.

CLEVER DOG

MARKING TERRITORY

When a male dog lifts its leg to the go to loo, it's a sign of dominance and a way of showing its status in the canine world. Its urine is full of potent scent markers, which alert other dogs of its presence. It cocks its leg as high as it can in order to spread the scent as far as possible. Female dogs have also been known to lift their leg in this way. Although this is not as common, it often happens if they've strayed far from home. They will urinate frequently, squatting and raising one leg to the side in order to scent mark the territory.

NOVEMBER

CANINE MYTH

INUGAMI

This mythical Japanese dog spirit has a cruel creation story. According to Japanese folklore, this vengeful beast is made when an owner buries their dog up to its neck, leaving it to die. Once the dog has passed on to the spirit world, it becomes indebted to its owner, despite the horrible circumstances of its death. Some myths suggest the owner may pay tribute to the dog, and present it with gifts of food to petition its spiritual support. Such is the loyalty of this spectral canine that it will guard and protect the family home from which it came, and also bless the inhabitants with wealth and good fortune.

Inugamis are believed to do the bidding of their owner, and can bestow curses on people who have wronged their family. But in some tales, they turn upon their creator and place a curse on them. Sometimes, the dog's spirit will try to return to its body, but if this is no longer available, it will find the next best thing and possess its human master or mistress. As unpleasant as this sounds, should an Inugami inhabit the body, it has the ability to cure any illness and bless a human with a long and healthy life.

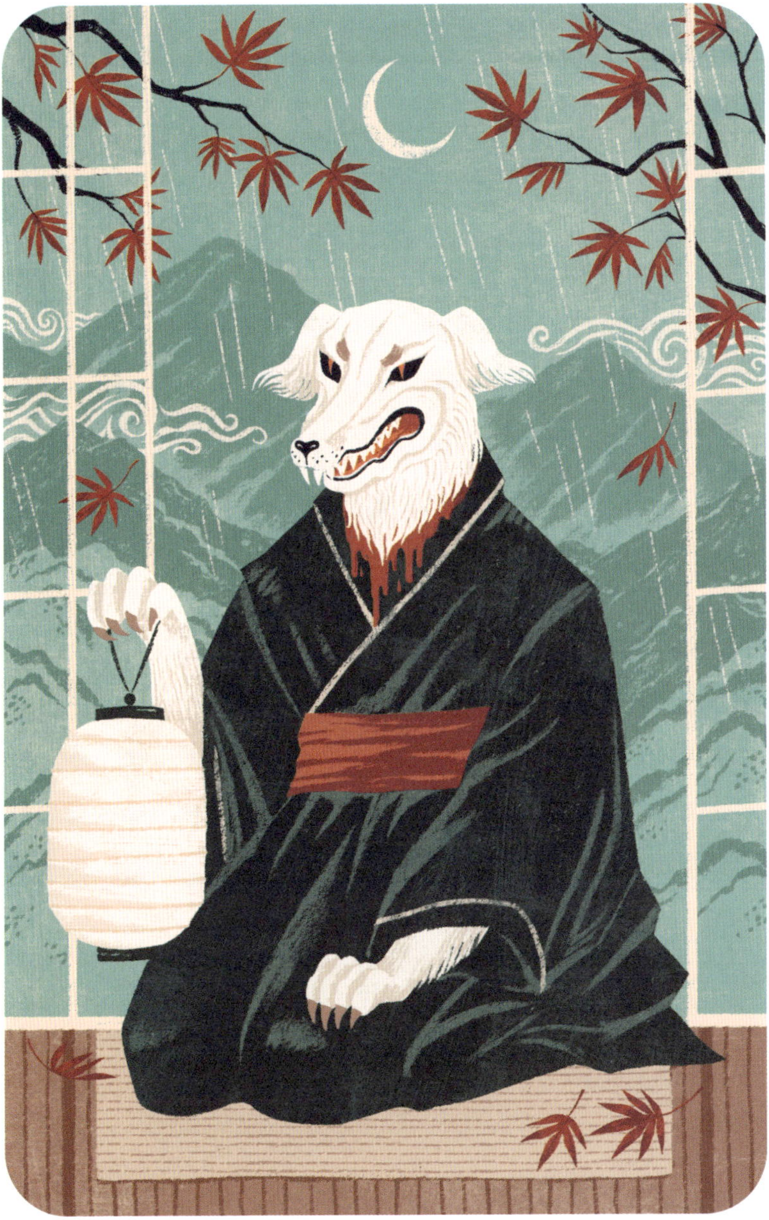

NOVEMBER

CANINE CHAT
LIPS AND LICKS

Dogs can't talk like us, but they do use their mouth, lips and tongue to tell you how they're feeling. A jaw that is relaxed with the mouth hanging wide open means your pup is in its happy place. This expression says, 'I feel fine.' If, however, their mouth is tightly shut, then a dog may feel closed off and wary. Should a pooch start avidly licking its lips and nose and it isn't during or after a meal, they may be feeling anxious about something. But if they're licking you, it's 'I love you' all the way. Yawning, doesn't necessarily mean tiredness, and can be a fear response, and your dog's way of saying 'go away'. If it's swiftly followed by a lip curl, then be warned: this dog is up for a fight.

PUPPY POWER MOVES
GENTLE JOG

Dogs are built for exercise and can run at speed. A quick race gives them a burst of energy and gets their tail wagging. While we can't get down and run on all fours, we can embrace the spirit of the sprint with some on-the-spot running and mindful breathing.

You can do this exercise inside or outside in your garden where you can actually move around. Make sure you have plenty of room before you begin, and do a few simple stretches to get your body ready. You may find that your dog wants to join in with this activity, and keep you motivated.

- Start with a gentle jog on the spot, and count the steps 'one, two' in your head.
- Keep your breath steady and pay attention to the rhythm.
- Gradually pick up speed so that the jog becomes more of a run.
- Breathe in through your nose, feeling your chest expand, then hold on to your breath. Then, exhale slowly through pursed lips.
- Continue for a few minutes, then gradually reduce the tempo until you come to a stop.

NOVEMBER

DOG FUN
STAY STIMULATED

Rotation of games is key if you want to keep your dog happy. Changing things up on a regular basis stimulates their brain, particularly if your pup gets bored easily. Keep dog toys tucked away and take out just a handful at a time. Let them play with these toys, then after a couple of days switch them with others and watch as your dog delights in discovering new playthings. This is a great way to keep things interesting while saving you the money of buying new toys. You can do the same when you're feeding them. Split up a selection of treats and dried biscuits and deposit them around the house in different spots so that your pup has to hunt for them. After a few days, change this up and use different feeding spots.

NOVEMBER

DOG SPELL

SPELL TO HELP YOUR DOG SETTLE INTO A NEW HOME

A home move is stressful for everyone, but even more so for your dog, who doesn't know what's going on. Not only is the new environment strange, but it will be filled with unfamiliar scents, which may put your pup on edge. To ease the process, try this cleansing ritual, which should fill your potential home with fresh, inviting energy.

You will need: a knife and chopping board, a handful of fresh sage, a small bowl, hot water, your dog's collar

Perform this spell if you can before your dog moves into your new home. If that's not possible, keep your dog in one room while you cleanse the rest of the space.

- Chop up the sage to release its herby scent, then put it into the bowl. Sage is associated with spiritual cleansing and has uplifting properties.
- Cover the sage with hot water, but only half-fill the bowl so that you can carry it easily from room to room.
- Walk to the first room of your house, wafting the steam around the space. Place the bowl on a window ledge or the floor and say, 'I cleanse this space of negativity. May it be warm and welcoming for my dog and me.'
- Move through your home, going from room to room, repeating this process as you go.

WINTER

The dark nights turn into darker days, and the sun's light slips even further away as winter comes calling. The chill seeps beneath the skin and bones of the earth, causing a hardening. But this brittleness has a beauty all of its own. While the trees stand like skeletal stalagmites upon the landscape, their stark appearance cuts through the gloom. Icy tendrils shimmer against a backdrop of silver and grey, and the frost adds a thin gauze of mystery to everything. No wonder winter walks are imbued with a little extra magic.

Longer-haired dog breeds are usually fine with the shift in temperature, and most pups prepare naturally by donning a thicker coat of fur to keep them toasty. But some smaller, thinner-coated breeds struggle. It's time to get those winter woollies and belly-warming coats ready for your canine companion.

Murky mornings and dark shadowy nights bring their own problems, so think about a fluorescent harness or high visibility vest to make your fur buddy visible. Some dogs love snow, diving nose-deep into the nearest flurry, but these can be deeper than they appear. The same goes for iced-up rivers and lakes, which may look solid, but can easily crumble under four paws. Once home, a brisk towel-dry and blanketed cuddle should keep the chill from setting in, but don't forget to provide lots of snug heated spots, especially for older arthritic hounds who need a bit of extra help at this time of year.

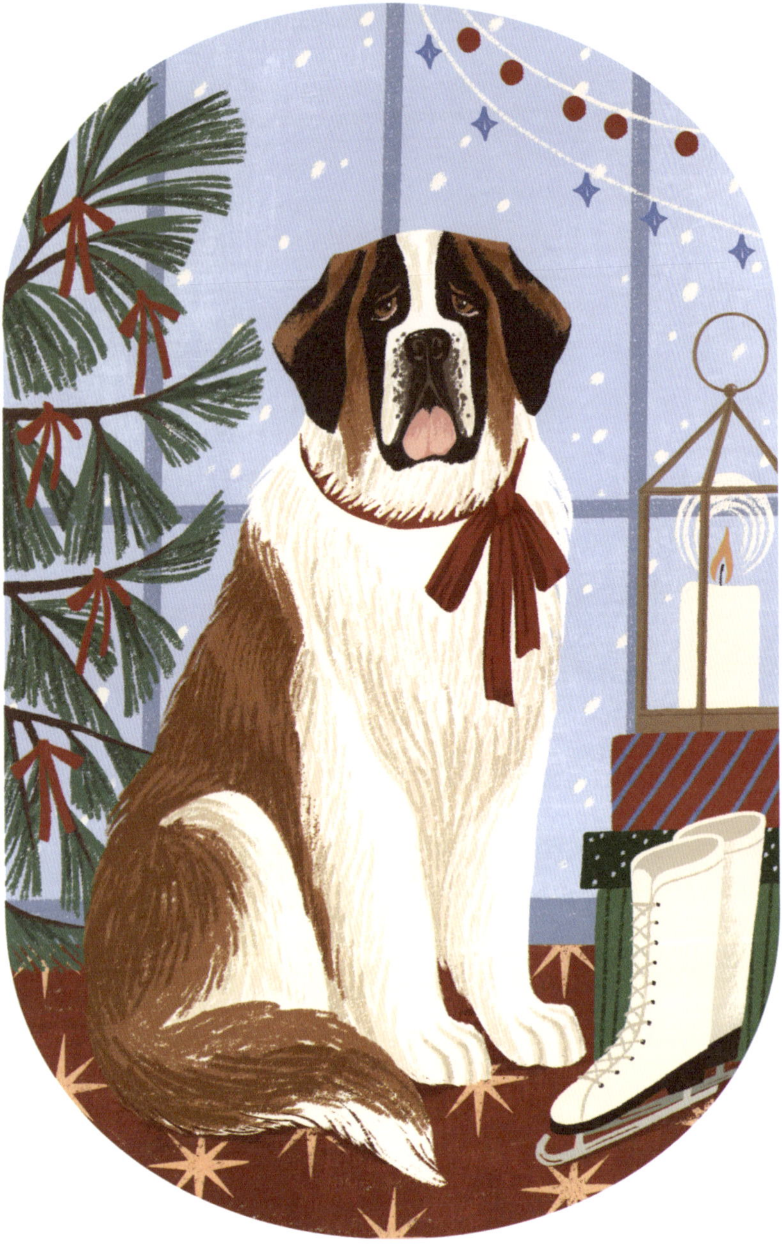

DECEMBER

DECEMBER

DOG OF THE MONTH

SAINT BERNARD

These gentle giants of the dog world have a reputation that matches their size. With a bulky, muscular frame and a large wrinkled head, their distinctive appearance sets them apart from other breeds. Jowls and loose lips mean there's a surplus of drool, but this is a small price to pay for a patient, loving partner in crime.

The national dog of Switzerland and something of a hero, the Saint Bernard started life as a Molosser, a mastiff-like breed brought over by the Romans around two thousand years ago. After settling in the Alps, these dogs mingled with local mountain dogs, and the outcome was a large working dog with a willing-to-please temperament.

Local monks wasted little time setting them to work, and while some dogs might have struggled with the harsh conditions, the Saint Bernard excelled. These hefty beauties get their name from the monk Bernard de Menthon, who famously cleared the treacherous stretch of land formerly known as the Mont-Joux Pass (now the Great St Bernard Pass). A notorious hideout for thieves and looters, the pass was covered in layers of snow and ice, but de Menthon made it safer and set up a hospice there. In later years, the Saint Bernard was used to guard the area and as companions for the residents. Over time, they proved their worth by making excellent rescue dogs with the ability to detect and dig out a person buried deep beneath the snow.

DECEMBER

DOG SUPERSTITION
HOUND HUES

Dogs come in all shapes, sizes and hues, and the colour of a dog's coat often crops up in superstitions. Golden-haired dogs are associated with wealth and abundance, and should one pay you lots of attention, it's likely you'll be blessed with prosperity. White dogs are often linked to love and romance, while black dogs, though generally feared and associated with death, also have strong links with protection, particularly of the family home. Symbolically, grey dogs are thought to be calm and wise, and brown dogs are linked to happiness. Brown dogs also have the ability to turn your luck around. For example, seeing an ambulance in Russia is considered a bad omen, but you can reverse the effects by holding your breath until you see a brown dog crossing the road.

CLEVER DOG
CANINE EVOLUTION

Dogs evolved from a now-extinct species of wolf. Their wild ancestors had bigger claws and paws, larger skulls and teeth equipped for catching and eating prey. As the dog emerged, it changed shape and became more obedient in its behaviour. According to research and the discovery of certain fossils, it's thought that by the Bronze Age there were likely five distinct types of dogs in existence. These were Mastiff-like creatures; a dog that closely resembled the wolf; a type of slender greyhound; herding dogs; and a pointed shaped canine. Today, it's a very different picture with around 360 dog breeds in the world.

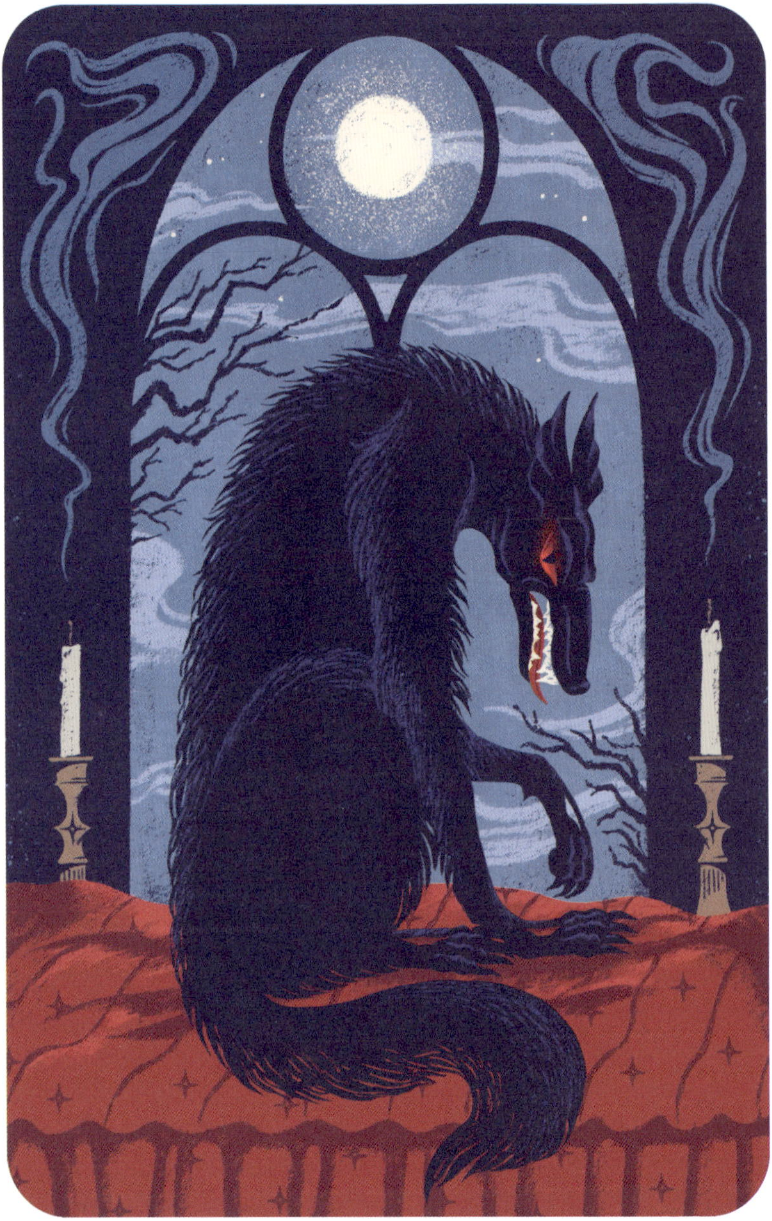

CANINE MYTH

THE PESANTA

Dark as the night, the skulking presence of the Pesanta lurks in the shadows. This enormous black dog of Catalan descent favours churches and old ruins as its hideout. According to Spanish folklore, it emerges at the dead of night when it sneaks into the home of its unsuspecting victims. Some believe it has the ability to slip beneath the door frame or pass through the keyhole like mist. With enormous paws made of steel and a thick shaggy coat, the Pesanta is a fearsome sight. But it has one weakness: each paw has a hole at its centre so that it cannot grip or steal anything.

Once in the home, it seeks out the owner and sits upon their chest while they sleep, making it almost impossible to breathe and serving up terrible nightmares. If the person awakes, the Pesanta will flee at such a speed that only its shadow is left behind. It's thought that you can keep a Pesanta at bay if you spread a layer of millet on your bedroom floor. While this dog may be wily, it's easily tricked, and rumours abound of a person avoiding an attack by persuading the beast to count all of the stars in the sky.

DECEMBER

CANINE CHAT
MAN'S BEST FRIEND

Dogs may not be able to speak, but they still have several ways of saying, 'I love you,' from snuggling up and leaning purposely against you, to bringing you their favourite toy. These little gestures are your pup's way of saying, 'You're the best!' Gazing lovingly into your eyes while lifting and wiggling their eyebrows is a top sign of affection, as is licking your face and generally making a fuss of you. It's all about being as close to you as possible, and following you around and sleeping next to you is their way of saying, 'You're my human and I think you're lovely.'

PUPPY POWER MOVES

SUPINE TWIST AND STRETCH

Dogs are fidgets in furry form. They twist and stretch, forming many different shapes that are similar to yoga moves. The supine spinal twist is one position that you'll often see your pooch perfect. It's great for releasing any tension in your back muscles, and can help to improve flexibility and digestion.

You will need: a yoga mat

- Start by laying on your back with your arms stretched out to the sides.

- Take a deep breath in and slowly bring your right knee up to your chest.

- As you exhale, let the right knee fall over to the left, keeping your left leg as straight as possible.

- Place your left hand on your right knee and apply some gentle pressure.

- Hold this position for three or four breaths, then roll back on to your back.

- Repeat on the other side

DECEMBER

DOG FUN

FESTIVE PUPS

The festive season can be hectic, and your pup will want to be front and centre of the action, so don't forget to include them in the fun. Whether you're wrapping up presents or giving your home a glitzy makeover, get your pooch involved. If you have any leftover bits of wrapping paper, scrunch them up into paper balls that they can chase. Or, fill an empty cardboard box with layers of papers and throw a few of their favourite treats into the mix, then watch them dive in and sniff out the goodies. Be sure to remove any staples or sticky tape before you start to make everything pup-friendly.

DECEMBER

DOG SPELL

SPELL TO CONNECT WITH A DOG WHO HAS PASSED ON

It's heartbreaking when any pet passes, but this simple spell will help you reach out to your lost loved one in the spirit world, connect with their energy, and send them a message of love.

You will need: a pin, a white tealight, a fire-safe dish, some frankincense essential oil, a lighter or matches

It's best to perform this spell on a Sunday when you can harness the sun's heartwarming energy.

- Take the pin and carve your pup's name, nickname, or, if you don't have much space, first letter of their name into the tealight.

- Sprinkle a couple of drops of the frankincense oil on the top of the tealight, and make sure it's securely placed in a fire-safe dish. This festive scent is associated with positive energy and helps to send joyful loving feelings out into the Universe.

- Light the candle and spend a few minutes gazing into the flame.

- As you feel more relaxed, bring your pooch to mind and recall a happy memory that you shared together. Know that they are with you in spirit, and send them your love.

- If you have a specific message, or anything you want to ask them, do it now by speaking it out loud or in your head.

- Breathe deeply in and out, relax and let the candle burn down naturally.

GLOSSARY OF MYSTICAL TERMS

ANCIENTS
People who lived thousands of years ago, who practised customs and traditions that tied into their beliefs

CANDLE MAGIC
A spell that uses a candle, or candles, to manifest a particular outcome

CHARM
An object imbued with specific magical energy, like a lucky coin, stone or crystal

CLEANSING
The spiritual practice of clearing negative energy from a space or the body's aura

DEITY
A supernatural being, also known as a god or goddess, that is considered divine or sacred

FOLKLORE
Stories, beliefs and customs, which are adopted by a culture and passed down through the generations

MEDICINE
The healing power associated with an animal, herb or flower

MOON PHASE
The term used to describe the changing shape of the moon in the sky

OMEN
A sign, either good or bad, which foretells the future

OTHERWORLD
A spiritual realm that exists alongside our own. Often used to describe the fairy realm

RITUAL
A series of magical actions performed in a set sequence. This can include gestures, words and actions, and the use of specific ingredients

SIXTH SENSE
A psychic sense, also called intuition, that relies on gut feelings and instincts

SPELL
A wish to bring about change that combines intention with energy, and sometimes uses external ingredients and words

SUPERSTITION
A belief or practice based on supernatural forces

SYMBOL
A sign, mark or shape that has particular meaning or is associated with an idea or belief

VISUALIZATION
The ability to see and picture what you would like to manifest in your mind

WANING
The term used to describe the moon phase as it is getting smaller in the sky

WAXING
The term used to describe the moon phase as it is getting bigger in the sky

DOG GLOSSARY

BARK
Sharp, shrill sound made by a dog for attention

CANINE
From the Canidae family which includes dogs, foxes, jackals and wolves etc.

HOWL
An eerie call that a dog makes

JOWLS
Loose skin that hangs down from a dog's jaw

LITTER
A group of puppies born to the same mother

MARKING
When a dog marks its territory using the scent in its urine

POOCH
Another name for a dog

PUP OR PUPPY
A young dog

RABIES
A rare but deadly virus that affects mammals

SNOOT/SNOUT
Another name for a dog's nose

STRAY
A dog with no home, usually living on the streets

WAG
Movement made by a dog's tail when they're happy

WALKIES
A term used to describe a regular walking session

WOOF
Sound a dog makes, not as harsh as a bark

YELP
High pitched barking sound, usually indicating distress

ZOOMIES
Random periods of racing around, when a dog is in high spirits

ABOUT THE AUTHOR

A professional storyteller with a keen interest in mythology, spirituality and the natural world, Alison Davies is the author of more than 60 books, including *The Cat Year*, *The Mystical Year*, *The Self-Care Year* and *The Lunar Year*. She also runs writing workshops at universities across the United Kingdom.

ACKNOWLEDGEMENTS

I'd like to thank my wonderful editors Sofie Shearman and Harriet Thornley for their help in creating this gorgeous book. A huge thank you goes out to the rest of the team at Quadrille – and my amazing copy editor Chloe Murphy, who weaved her 'magic' once again to make my words shine. Finally, I'd like to give a special thank you to the amazingly talented illustrator Anastasia for her fantastic artwork which brings to life each pup and pooch on the page. I hope this book captures the joy and enthusiasm that our canine friends conjure each day!

MANAGING DIRECTOR
Sarah Lavelle

PROJECT EDITORS
Sofie Shearman
Harriet Thornley

SERIES DESIGNER
Emily Lapworth

DESIGNER
Katy Everett

ILLUSTRATOR
Anastasia Stefurak

HEAD OF PRODUCTION
Stephen Lang

SENIOR PRODUCTION CONTROLLER
Martina Georgieva

COPY EDITOR
Chloe Murphy

Quadrille, Penguin Random House UK, One Embassy Gardens,
8 Viaduct Gardens, London SW11 7BW

Quadrille Publishing Limited is part of the Penguin Random
House group of companies whose addresses can be found at
global.penguinrandomhouse.com

Penguin
Random House
UK

Text © Alison Davies 2025
Illustrations © Anastasia Stefurak 2025
Compilation, design and layout © Quadrille 2025

No part of this book may be used or reproduced in any manner
for the purpose of training artificial intelligence technologies or
systems. In accordance with Article 4(3) of the DSM Directive 2019/790,
Penguin Random House expressly reserves this work from the text and
data mining exception.

Published by Quadrille in 2025

www.penguin.co.uk

A CIP catalogue record for this book is available from the British Library

ISBN 978 1 83783 278 1

10 9 8 7 6 5 4 3 2 1

Colour reproduction by p2d

Printed in China by C&C Offset Printing Co., Ltd.

The authorised representative in the EEA is Penguin Random House
Ireland, Morrison Chambers, 32 Nassau Street, Dublin D02 YH68.

MIX
Paper | Supporting
responsible forestry
FSC® C018179

Penguin Random House is committed to a sustainable future for
our business, our readers and our planet. This book is made from
Forest Stewardship Council® certified paper.